Cost-Benefit Analysis of Special and Incentive Pays for Career Enlisted Aviators

PATRICIA K. TONG, MICHAEL G. MATTOCK, BETH J. ASCH

Prepared for the Department of the Air Force
Approved for public release; distribution unlimited

RAND PROJECT AIR FORCE

For more information on this publication, visit www.rand.org/t/RRA189-1

Library of Congress Cataloging-in-Publication Data is available for this publication.
ISBN: 978-1-9774-0606-4

Published by the RAND Corporation, Santa Monica, Calif.

Cover: B-29 flight engineer: Tech. Sgt. Alexander Riedel/509th Bomb Wing Public Affairs.

Preface

The research discussed in this report was conducted as part of an effort to develop a capability to determine the efficient amount of special and incentive (S&I) pay for U.S. Air Force career enlisted aviators (CEAs). The research extends and estimates the RAND Corporation's Dynamic Retention Model for CEAs by specialty and runs simulations showing the effects of changes to special and incentive (S&I) pays on retention. A second goal was to incorporate the cost of recruiting and training CEAs by specialty, show the trade-off between estimated recruiting and training costs and retention costs, and calculate tipping-point values—that is, the values that recruiting and training costs would need to reach before retaining experienced CEAs becomes more cost-effective than increasing accessions. This project should be of interest to those concerned with the effect of S&I pays on retention.

The research reported here was sponsored by AF/A1P and conducted within the Manpower, Personnel, and Training Program of RAND Project AIR FORCE as part of a project entitled "Cost-Benefit Analysis of Special and Incentive Pays for Aviators."

RAND Project AIR FORCE

RAND Project AIR FORCE (PAF), a division of the RAND Corporation, is the Department of the Air Force's (DAF's) federally funded research and development center for studies and analyses, supporting both the United States Air Force and the United States Space Force. PAF provides DAF with independent analyses of policy alternatives affecting the development, employment, combat readiness, and support of current and future air, space, and cyber forces. Research is conducted in four programs: Strategy and Doctrine; Force Modernization and Employment; Manpower, Personnel, and Training; and Resource Management. The research reported here was prepared under contract FA7014-16-D-1000.

Additional information about PAF is available on our website:

www.rand.org/paf/

This report documents work originally shared with DAF on December 10, 2019. The draft report, issued on March 25, 2020 was reviewed by formal peer reviewers and DAF subject-matter experts.

Contents

Figures

Tables

Summary

Issue

The U.S. Air Force is required to justify budgets for special and incentive (S&I) pays for career enlisted aviators (CEAs). To do so, the Air Force needs rigorous analyses on how to efficiently set S&I pays for CEAs to achieve and maintain required end strength, where the efficient S&I pay levels account for the retention responses of CEAs to changes in these pays.

Approach

We expanded the RAND Corporation's Dynamic Retention Model (DRM) to create separate models for each CEA specialty. These models allow for simulations under different S&I pay regimes. We used these models to estimate the per capita cost for each CEA specialty under different policies to show the trade-offs between retaining CEAs and increasing accessions for a given force size. We also used these models to calculate *tipping-point values*: the values that recruiting and training costs would need to reach before retaining experienced CEAs using selective reenlistment bonuses (SRBs) becomes more cost-effective than increasing accessions.

Conclusions

- If a more experienced CEA force is needed, then increasing SRBs is more cost-effective than increasing Critical Skills Incentive Pay (CSIP).
- Holding force size constant, increasing SRBs causes the composition of CEAs to change by increasing the proportion of more experienced CEAs.
- The trade-off between increasing SRBs to retain CEAs and increasing accessions to sustain a given CEA force size depends on recruiting and training costs. Given available data on recruiting and training costs, we find that, with the exception of a subset of Flight Engineers, increasing accessions is more efficient than increasing SRBs to sustain a given force size.
- For Flight Engineers who are training to be part of the flight crew on CV-22 aircraft, retaining more experienced personnel using SRBs is more efficient than increasing accessions to sustain force size if SRB multipliers are below 2.5, whereas increasing accessions is more efficient if SRB multipliers are above 2.5.

Implications

- When recruiting and training costs are low, increasing accessions is more cost-effective than increasing retention via SRBs.
- Once recruiting and training costs exceed certain values, it becomes more cost-effective to increase SRBs and have a more experienced CEA force than to increase the training

pipeline to sustain force size. With the exception of Flight Engineers on CV-22 aircraft, estimated recruiting and training costs would have to increase substantially before they exceed these tipping-cost values, as show in Table S.1.

- For CV-22 Flight Engineers, estimated recruiting and training costs are sufficiently close to the estimated tipping point that increasing SRBs and increasing accessions to sustain a given force size cost could be considered approximately the same. This finding suggests that the Air Force could be indifferent between the two options from a cost standpoint.

Table S.1. Comparison of Recruiting and Training Costs and Tipping Points, by Career Enlisted Aviator Occupation, 2018

Career Enlisted Aviator	Estimated Recruiting and Training Costs	Tipping Points
In-Flight Refueling (1A0)	$289,805	$585,000
Flight Engineers (1A1)	$251,583 (C-130H) to $1,559,003 (CV-22)	$1,485,000
Aircraft Loadmasters (1A2)	$113,692 (C-130J) to $316,301 (C-17)	$580,000
Airborne Mission Systems Operators (1A3)	$47,964	$720,000
Airborne Cryptologists (1A8X1)	$85,812 (Spanish) to $194,024 (Arabic)	$1,015,000
Special Missions Aviation (1A9)	$36,402	$1,500,000

SOURCE: The estimated recruiting and training costs come from Table 18-1a and Table 35-1 in Air Force Instruction 65-503 and were scaled up to 2018 dollars.

Acknowledgments

We are grateful for the support of our project sponsor, Maj Gen Robert D. LaBrutta (AF/A1P). We also benefited from the input and support of our project monitor, Lt Col Dale W. Stanley III, Chief, Rated Force Policy (HQ USAF/A1PP), and from CMSgt Philip P. Leonard, Chief, Career Enlisted Aviator CFM (HQ USAF/A3TF), and SMSgt Eric M. Gaul, Chief, (HQ USAF/A3TF) We are also grateful for the help we received from several of our RAND colleagues, including Anthony Lawrence and Paul Emslie. Our report benefited from the reviews we received from John Ausink and Matt Walsh at RAND. Finally, we would like to thank Ray Conley and Kirsten Keller, director and associate director, respectively, of the Manpower, Personnel, and Training Program within RAND Project AIR FORCE.

Abbreviations

AFI	Air Force Instruction
AFSC	Air Force Specialty Code
AvIP	aviation incentive pay
BRS	blended retirement system
CEA	career enlisted aviator
CFETP	Career Field Education and Training Plan
CSIP	Critical Skills Incentive Pay
DMDC	Defense Manpower Data Center
DoD	U.S. Department of Defense
DRM	dynamic retention model
FLPB	foreign language proficiency bonus
FY	fiscal year
NCP	normal cost percentage
OUSD(C)	Office of the Under Secretary of Defense (Comptroller)
OUSD(P&R)	Office of the Under Secretary of Defense for Personnel and Readiness
PAF	RAND Project AIR FORCE
RMC	regular military compensation
RPA	remotely piloted aircraft
S&I	special and incentive
SRB	selective reenlistment bonus
TAFMS	total active federal military service
WEX	Work Experience File
YAS	year(s) of aviation service
YOS	year(s) of service

1. Introduction

Career enlisted aviators (CEAs) are the U.S. Air Force's enlisted flight crewmembers. CEAs include Flight Engineers, Aircraft Loadmasters, Flight Attendants, Airborne Mission Systems Operators, and Airborne Cryptologists, among other career fields; the full list is shown in Table 1.1.[1] These enlisted personnel are part of the in-flight crew on certain aircraft and provide a number of mission-critical functions. For example, flight engineers oversee the safe functioning of a variety of aircraft systems, and loadmasters ensure that cargo loads are within weight limits and distributed properly.

Table 1.1. Career Enlisted Aviator Occupations

Occupation Title	5-Digit Air Force Specialty Code
In-Flight Refueling (Boom Operators)	1A0X1
Flight Engineers	1A1X1
Aircraft Loadmaster	1A2X1
Airborne Mission System Operator	1A3X1
Flight Attendant	1A6X1
Airborne Cryptologic Language Analyst	1A8X1
Airborne Intelligence, Surveillance, and Reconnaissance (ISR) Operator	1A8X2
Special Missions Aviation	1A9X1
Remotely Piloted Aircraft (RPA) Sensor Operator	1U0X1
Enlisted RPA Pilot	1U1XX

Special and incentive (S&I) pays are used by the Air Force to promote CEA retention so that it can compete with civilian job opportunities available to its CEAs, especially since many CEA skills are transferable to the civilian sector. The Air Force is required to justify budgets for S&I pays for CEAs and needs rigorous analyses on how to efficiently set these pays to achieve and maintain desired inventory levels. Furthermore, because an alternative approach to achieving a given inventory of CEAs is to recruit more CEAs rather than to retain those already in service, the Air Force requires analysis of the return on investment from increasing S&I pays versus spending more to expand the training pipeline and train more CEAs. That is, it requires an analysis of the trade-off between (1) increasing CEA accessions and incurring greater recruiting

[1] A description of these occupations and the training and experiences required to be mission-ready is provided in Appendix A, drawing from Chapter 2 of Tong et al. (2020).

and training costs and (2) increasing retention and incurring higher S&I pay costs, as well as higher personnel costs associated with a more senior force.

To ensure that the Air Force uses its resources efficiently to sustain the CEA force, the Air Force asked RAND Project AIR FORCE (PAF) to estimate the retention and cost effects of changing S&I pays for each CEA specialty. The Air Force also requested that PAF provide information on the efficient amount of S&I pays for CEAs, accounting for the trade-offs between retaining CEAs through the use of S&I pays and increasing accessions for a fixed force size.

In this report, we examine the impact of increasing accessions and S&I pays on retention and costs. Specifically, we focus on two types of S&I pays: Critical Skills Incentive Pay (CSIP) and selective reenlistment bonuses (SRBs). All CEAs are currently eligible for CSIP, which provides additional compensation that is paid to members performing flight duty. SRBs vary across the CEA career fields, or Air Force Specialty Codes (AFSCs), and provide additional financial incentives to reenlist. These SRBs vary in size based on the fiscal year and the AFSC. These three policy levers are summarized in Table 1.2.

Table 1.2. Policy Levers

Policy Levers	Description
Critical Skills Incentive Pay (CSIP)	Monthly benefit paid for regular and frequent flying. Benefit varies with years of aviation service (YAS).
Selective reenlistment bonuses (SRBs)	Benefit tied to a service agreement to target career fields with low retention and/or high training costs.
Accessions	Increasing training pipeline.

The first step in our approach is summarized in Tong et al. (2020). That report summarizes the estimation of models of CEA retention. These models are the foundation of the analytic capability for assessing the efficiency of S&I pays presented in this report. In particular, in that earlier report, we estimate models of retention for In-Flight Refueling, Aircraft Loadmasters, and Airborne Mission Systems Operators. These three CEA specialties share similar retention profiles and make up over half of the CEA population among the cohorts included in the study summarized in this report. Tong et al. (2020) also provides contextual information on the CEA specialties, including background on the S&I pays that have historically been offered to these specialties.

The analysis summarized in this report builds on this first step. In the analysis presented here, we extend RAND's Dynamic Retention Model (DRM) to allow analysis of CEA retention by specialty and we then estimate these AFSC-specific models. These estimated models extend the model presented in Tong et al. (2020) in two ways. First, we estimate models for each CEA specialty for which we have sufficient data, not just In-Flight Refueling, Aircraft Loadmasters, and Airborne Mission Systems Operators. Second, the models we estimate in this phase of the study incorporate S&I pays and specifically the S&I pays the Air Force offered historically to each CEA in our data. We then use the model estimates for each specialty to conduct simulations of the retention and cost effects of changes in S&I pays. We also use the model simulations to estimate the trade-off between retaining CEAs through the use of S&I pays and increasing accessions for a fixed force size. These trade-offs are based on estimated recruiting and training costs that rely on certain assumptions. Using these estimated trade-offs, we calculate tipping-point values to show the values of recruiting and training costs that would be required before retaining experienced CEAs becomes more cost-effective than increasing accessions.

The remainder of this report is organized as follows. In Chapter 2, we present an overview of the DRM; describe the data used; present the CEA-specific DRM models, including the parameter estimates and model fits; and demonstrate the models' simulation capabilities by considering different S&I pay regimes. In Chapter 3, we present the analysis comparing the costs of retaining CEAs with the costs of expanding the training pipeline. In Chapter 4, we provide our conclusions. We provide background information on the CEA specialties in Appendix A, and Appendix B shows observed retention profiles for each CEA specialty. Finally, Appendix C provides simulation results of the retention and cost effects of varying S&I pays for each CEA specialty for which we estimate a model.

2. Dynamic Retention Model Overview, Data, Estimates, and Model Fits

RAND's Dynamic Retention Model (DRM) is well suited for the analysis of structural changes in military compensation, such as changes in S&I pays for CEAs. In this chapter, we provide a brief overview of the DRM and the data we use to estimate the model. We then present the model estimates and show how well the models fit the observed retention behavior for different CEA AFSCs. The DRM has been described in detail in earlier documents, including a DRM for officers and for enlisted personnel in each service (Asch et al., 2008) and for selected communities such as military mental health care providers (Hosek et al., 2017) and Air Force pilots, (Mattock et al., 2016). We have also estimated a DRM for a subset of CEA AFSCs (Tong et al., 2020). The analysis presented in this report extends the CEA DRM model to create separate AFSC specific models for In-Flight Refueling, Flight Engineers, Aircraft Loadmasters, Airborne Mission Systems Operators, Airborne Cryptologists, Special Mission Aviation, and Remotely Piloted Aircraft (RPA) Sensor Operators.[2] It also extends our earlier work on CEAs by incorporating into the DRM the historical offering of S&I pays to CEAs by the Air Force.

Conceptual Overview

The DRM is based on a mathematical model of individual decisionmaking over the life cycle of the individual in a world with uncertainty and in which members have heterogeneous preferences (tastes) for active and reserve service. The model begins with service in the active component, and individuals make a decision to stay or leave each year. Those who leave the active component take a civilian job and, at the same time, choose whether to participate in a reserve component. The decision of whether to participate in a reserve component is made each year, and the individual can move into or out of the reserves from year to year. More specifically, a reservist can choose to remain in the reserves or leave the reserves to lead a purely civilian life, and a civilian can choose to enter the reserves or remain a civilian. The model assumes that individuals are forward-looking and anticipate being able to revisit the decision to stay or leave each year. The model is formulated in terms of parameters that are estimated with longitudinal administrative data on retention in the active component and participation in the reserve component. These estimated parameters are used to conduct policy simulations in which we alter S&I pays. In short, in the DRM, a set of parameters underlies the retention decisions, and one

---

[2] Due to small sample size, the following CEA AFSCs were excluded from the analysis: Flight Attendants (1A6), Airborne Intelligence, Surveillance, Reconnaissance Operators (1A8X2), and enlisted RPA pilots (1U1).

goal of our analysis is to use individual-level data on enlisted retention over their careers to estimate the parameters.

Individuals are assumed to differ in their preferences for serving in the military. Each enlisted Air Force member is assumed to have given, unobserved, time-invariant preferences for active and reserve service. Military pay, military retirement benefits, and civilian pay are known to the service member, meaning that the individual knows the trajectory of pay over a military and civilian career, as well as the trajectory of income in retirement. In each year, there are random shocks associated with each alternative, and the shocks affect the value of the alternative. The model explicitly accounts for individual preferences and military and civilian compensation, and shocks represent current-period conditions that affect the value of being on active duty, being in the selected reserve and being a civilian worker (*reserve* for short), or being a civilian worker and not in the selected reserve (*civilian* for short). The following factors are examples of what may contribute to a shock: a good assignment; a dangerous mission; an excellent leader; inadequate training or equipment for the tasks at hand; a strong or weak civilian job market; an opportunity for on-the-job training or promotion; the choice of location; a change in marital status, dependency status, or health status; the prospect of deployment or deployment itself; and a change in school tuition rates. These factors may affect the relative payoff of being in an active component, being in a reserve component, or being a civilian. The distribution of future shocks is unknown, meaning that individuals are not able to perfectly predict the types of shocks listed above. As a result, an individual uses the information that is realized in the current period to choose the option with the highest expected value. The combinations of preferences and shocks provides us flexibility to model different situations. For example, a person with a low preference for active duty could face a positive shock and decide to remain in active duty, and a person with a high preference for active duty could face a negative shock and decide to leave. The individual is assumed to know the distributions that generate the shocks and the shock realizations in the current period, but not in future periods.

The individual receives the pay associated with serving in the active component, working as a civilian, or serving in a reserve component and working as a civilian based on the alternative chosen. In addition, the individual receives the intrinsic monetary equivalent of the preference for serving in an active component or serving in a reserve component. These values are assumed to be relative to that of working as a civilian, which is set at zero.

Technical Overview

The model assumes that each individual begins in the active component. In each period, an individual can choose to continue or leave the active component. If they leave, they can then decide whether to hold only a civilian job or to both hold a civilian job and participate in the reserve component. Once the individual has left the active component, he or she cannot return; however, the individual can move back and forth between the reserve component and civilian states. In the equations below, superscript A/a represents values for being in the active component; superscript R/r represents values for being in the reserve component; superscript C/c represents values for being in the civilian sector; superscript S represents values for staying in the active component; and superscript L represent values for leaving the active component.

We denote the value of staying active at time *t* as

$$V_t^S = V_t^A + \epsilon_t^A,$$

where V_t^A is the nonstochastic value of the active alternative and ϵ_t^A is the random shock at time *t*. Similarly, the value of leaving at time *t* is

$$V_t^L = max[V_t^R + \omega_t^R, V_t^C + \omega_t^C] + \epsilon_t^L,$$

where the member can choose to enter the reserves or be a civilian. The member will decide to stay in the active component if the value of doing so is greater than the value of leaving for the reserves or the civilian sector.

We allow one common shock across the reserve and civilian nest, ϵ_t^L, since an individual in the reserves also holds a civilian job, as well as two shock terms that are specific to the reserve and civilian sectors, ω_t^R and ω_t^C. The distributions of the shocks are time-invariant and are known; the shocks in the current period are known, but are not known in future periods, only the shock distributions are known in future periods. Once a future period has been reached and the shocks are realized, the individual can reoptimize (i.e., choose the alternative with the maximum value at that time). Additional technical details about the DRM can be found in Asch, Hosek, and Mattock (2013).

The value of the alternatives, V_t^A, V_t^R, and V_t^C depend on the current-period pay associated with serving in an active component or working as a civilian, W_t^a or W_t^c. If the individual is a reservist, they earn the civilian wage plus reserve pay, $W_t^c + W_t^r$. In addition, each individual has a "taste" for active and reserve duty, γ_a and γ_r, respectively, and these enter the value functions as well. Each taste represents the net advantage of holding an active or reserve position, relative to being a civilian. All else equal, a higher taste for active or reserve duty increases retention. These tastes are assumed to (1) be constant for each individual over time but may vary across individuals and (2) have a bivariate normal distribution across active and reserve component entrants. We estimate means in taste (denoted μ_a and μ_r for active and reserve duty, respectively), their standard deviations (denoted σ_a and σ_r), and the correlation between active and reserve tastes (denoted ρ).

The nonstochastic value of staying active can therefore be written as

$$V_t^A = \gamma_a + W_t^a + \beta E\left[max[V_{t+1}^L, V_{t+1}^S]\right],$$

where β is the personal discount factor. As described in Appendix A and in more detail below, CEAs are also eligible to receive S&I pays including CSIP and SRBs. These pays are included in our computation current period pay or W_t^a and future pay includes expected S&I pays.

The expected value of the best choice in the next period, $E\left[max[V_{t+1}^L, V_{t+1}^S]\right]$, and therefore the possibility of reoptimizing, is a key feature of dynamic programming models that distinguishes them from other dynamic models. In the current period, with future realizations unknown, the best the individual can do is to estimate the expected value of the best choice in the next period—i.e., the expected value of the maximum. Logically, this will also be true in the next period, and the one after it, and so forth, so the model is forward-looking and rationally handles future uncertainty. Moreover, the model presumes that the individual can reoptimize in each future period, depending on the state and shocks realized in that period. Thus, today's decision takes into account the possibility of future career changes and assumes that future decisions will also be optimizing.

The nonstochastic value of the reserve choice, V_t^R, can be written as

$$V_t^R = \gamma_r + W_t^c + W_t^r + \beta E\left[max[V_{t+1}^R + \omega_r, V_{t+1}^C + \omega_c]\right],$$

while the nonstochastic value of civilian choice is

$$V_t^C = W_t^c + R_t + \beta E\left[max[V_{t+1}^R + \omega_r, V_{t+1}^C + \omega_c]\right],$$

where R_t in the civilian equation is the value of any active or reserve military retirement benefit for which the individual is eligible.

Switching Costs

To assist with modeling movement from the active component to the reserves or civilian sector and movement between the reserves and civilian sector, we include switching costs as parameters to be estimated by the model. These costs are not paid by the individual but are implicit costs that are included in the model when making certain transitions. They allow the model to account for differences in costs associated with leaving active duty service before and after the first term, as well as movement from the active component to the reserve component. For example, because members who fail to complete the service obligation associated with receipt of an SRB are required to repay the bonus on a pro-rated basis, the switching costs include the pro-rated repayment required for those who do not complete their service obligation. Switching costs also include implicit costs, such as the difficulty with finding an available reserve position for which the member is qualified in the desired geographic location, particularly when not transitioning directly from active duty. The observed retention profiles by years of service (YOS) vary across the CEAs by specialty, so the set of switching costs included in the models also vary. The retention profiles are shown in Appendix B.

The models for In-flight Refueling (1A0), Aircraft Loadmasters (1A2), Airborne Mission System Operators (1A3), and Special Mission Aviation (1A9) have four switching costs. These costs are based on the observed retention patterns over a career for these occupations that show drops in retention among active component personnel and increases in reserve participation at 4 YOS (Figures B.1, B.3, B.4, and B.6). The first switching cost is the cost of leaving active duty service for a civilian job before completing 4 YOS. The second and third costs are specified to model the movement from active duty to the reserves. In particular, the second is the cost of moving from active to reserve duty before completing 4 years of active duty service, and the third is the cost of moving from active to reserve duty after completing 4 or more years of active duty service. The fourth is the cost of moving from a purely civilian state to participating in the reserves. We note that the retention profile for In-Flight Refueling (1A0) shows a drop in retention among active component personnel and an increase in reserve participation at 6 YOS (Figure B.1). We do not include additional switching costs to model this behavior, since the model with the four switching costs described above fit the observed data well, as shown in Figure 2.1.

The model for Airborne Cryptologists (1A8X1) includes the same switching costs as those for the aforementioned group except for the second cost, of moving from active to reserve duty before completing 4 years of active duty service. Airborne Cryptologists are different from this group in that their retention profiles do not show a jump to reserve duty at 4 YOS (Figure B.5). As a result, the cost associated with making this transition is excluded from its model.

Unlike the other CEAs, Flight Engineers are required to have prior experience in other AFSCs and historically had 5–6 YOS before becoming mission ready. This causes their observed retention profile to look different from those for the other CEAs, with near 100 percent retention until 6 YOS (Figure B.2). The model for Flight Engineers (1A1) includes two switching costs, one for the cost of moving from a civilian job to a reserve position and one for the cost for moving from active duty to the reserves.

We are limited to, at most, 10 years of observed data for RPA Sensor Operators. The active and reserve component retention figures for RPA Sensor Operators shown in Figure B.7 depict drops in active duty service and increases in reserve participation at YOS 4 and 6. To model these switches, we include six switching costs in the RPA Sensor Operator Model. The first is the cost of leaving active duty service for a civilian job before completing 4 YOS, and the second is the cost of leaving active duty service for a civilian job after completing 4 YOS but before finishing 6 YOS. The third, fourth, and fifth costs, respectively are specified to model movement from active to reserves before 4 years of active duty service, at 4 or 5 years of active duty service, and at 6 or more years of active duty service. The sixth switching cost is the cost of moving from a civilian job to a reserve position.

Data

There are two primary sources of data used for this project. Both sources of data come from the Defense Manpower Data Center (DMDC). The first source of data is the Work Experience File (WEX), which tracks the careers of service members from their date of entry. The WEX data are at the individual service member level and include information on the AFSC associated with members in each transactional record but do not include information about service member compensation or S&I pays.[3] The transactional records are aggregated to create files at an annual level for each service member present in a given year. The second data source used for this research are the Active Duty Pay Files. These data include monthly pay and compensation at the individual service member level, including S&I pays. However, the Active Duty Pay Files do not include information about the service member's AFSC. As a result, to identify S&I pays for CEAs, the two files were merged together using scrambled social security numbers.

For this project, we extracted WEX data for Air Force enlisted service members who entered from 1990 through 2000, with the exception of 1992, for which we denote entry year as cohort year, and we restrict the set of members to those who have a CEA AFSC recorded on their personnel record during their military tenure. The active and reserve service of each member entering during these years is tracked annually through 2012. The 1992 cohort is excluded because the active component retention profiles from that year were atypical compared to those for the other cohorts, for unknown reasons. Also, we do not track cohorts beyond 2012 because of recent "force shaping" by the Air Force that resulted in some enlisted personnel ending their active duty careers earlier than anticipated. Because of small sample size, the Special Missions Aviation model includes additional cohorts. Specifically, the Special Missions Aviation Model uses WEX data for cohorts 1990-1991 and 1993–2007 and follows them until 2012. RPA Sensor Operators is a relatively new career field, with those entering the occupation as direct accessions beginning in 2009 (as opposed to being retrained from other occupations). As a result, we use WEX data to follow the careers for the 2009 through 2013 cohorts until 2018. Given the short window of observed data, the RPA Sensor Operator model is exploratory, and RPA Sensor Operators are excluded from subsequent simulations and the analysis of the trade-off between retaining CEAs using S&I pays and increasing accessions.

We supplemented these data with information on active, reserve, and civilian pay. Active component pay, reserve component pay, and civilian pay are averages based on the individual's years of active, reserve, and total experience, respectively. We used 2007 military pay tables. Military pay increases are typically across-the-board, with the structure of pay by grade and year

[3] The WEX is a transactional file in which a new record is added every time one of eight variables changes (service, component, reserve category code, pay grade, primary service occupation code, secondary service occupation code, duty service occupation code, and unit identification).

of service remaining the same.[4] Therefore, we do not expect our results to be sensitive to the choice of year. Data on regular military compensation (RMC) and basic pay are from the *Selected Military Compensation Tables*, also known as the Greenbook (Office of the Under Secretary of Defense for Personnel and Readiness, Directorate of Compensation, 1980–2018). RMC includes basic pay, basic allowance for housing, basic allowance for subsistence, and the federal income tax advantage from the exclusion of the allowances from federal income tax. For civilian pay opportunities for enlisted personnel, we used the 2007 median wage for full-time male workers with associate's degrees.

Special and Incentive Pays

As discussed earlier in this chapter, the DRM for each model includes the S&I pays associated with each CEA. In particular, each CEA model includes CSIP and SRBs. The model for Airborne Cryptologists (1A8X1) also includes foreign language proficiency bonuses (FLPBs). The historical rates for and detailed descriptions of these S&I pays can be found in Tong et al. (2020). The specific rates of these S&I pays included in the model are based on historical values, and then scaled to 2007 dollars. For the simulations, we use 2018 S&I pay values and scale the military and civilian pay profiles to 2018 dollars.

Individuals with AFSCs of 1AXXX or 1UXXX are in training to receive these AFSCs and are eligible to receive CSIP if they are qualified for aviation service (Air Force Instruction [AFI] 11-421, 2018, p. 86). CSIP is paid either on a continuous basis or on a conditional month-to-month basis, in which they only receive payments if they perform regular and frequent flying duty in that month (more than four hours that month; AFI 11-401, 2018, p. 76). CSIP varies by years of aviation service (YAS), as shown in Table 2.1, with increases after 4, 8, and 14 YAS.

Table 2.1. Critical Skills Incentive Pay Rates for October 1, 2017 to Present

Years of Aviation Service	Monthly Pay
4 or less	$225
Over 4	$350
Over 8	$500
Over 14	$600

SOURCE: Office of the Under Secretary of Defense (Comptroller), 2018, Chapter 22.

SRBs are offered to enlisted personnel in certain career fields with low retention and/or high training costs. The SRB amounts and payment structures vary by zone (i.e., zones A, B, C, and

[4] An exception was the structural adjustment to the basic pay table in fiscal year (FY) 2000 that gave larger increases to midcareer personnel who had reached their pay grades relatively quickly (after fewer YOS). A second exception was the expansion of the basic allowance for housing, which increased in real value from FY 2000 to FY 2005. It should be noted that the costing analysis is in 2016 dollars.

E) where zones are determined by Total Active Federal Military Service (TAFMS), as shown in Table 2.2.

Table 2.2. Selective Reenlistment Bonus Schedule

SRB Eligibility Zone	Minimum TAFMS	Maximum TAFMS	Percentage of Total Amount Paid as Initial Lump Sum (FY 2017)
A	17 months	6 years	50%, then annual installments over agreed term of enlistment
B	6 years	10 years	75% then annual installments over agreed term of enlistment
C	10 years	14 years	100%
E	18 years	20 years	100%

SOURCE: AFI 36-2606, 2017, p. 45.

SRBs are calculated by multiplying a month's basic pay by the number of years reenlisting and by the SRB multiplier. These multipliers vary by AFSC and zone. Historical SRBs for Zones A, B, and C that are specific to each CEA AFSC are included in the model. Zone E is excluded since SRBs for Zone E were not available to CEAs modeled during the years covered by the data. For simplicity, we assume that the SRB for Zone A applies in YOS 4, the SRB for Zone B applies in YOS 8, and the SRB for Zone C applies in YOS 12. Historical SRB multipliers vary within the Flight Engineer community and Airborne Cryptologist community. For these two communities, we use the maximum historical SRB multiplier for a given year within each community.

FLPB are paid out on a monthly basis to airmen with qualifying language skills, and these monthly amounts vary by language. To include FLPB in the model for Airborne Cryptologists, we use the historical annual average amount of FLPB received among Airborne Cryptologists who received FLPB as compensation. To compute the conditional average amounts of FLPB over time for each CEA, we merged the WEX data with Active Duty Pay Files. These merged data include cohorts 1993 through 2002 and the extracts contained data through 2012. No Airborne Cryptologists were observed to have FLPB in the data in 1993. The conditional average FLPB amounts were calculated for years 1994 through 2012. To include FLPB in the Airborne Cryptologist model for years 1990–1993, the FLPB was set equal to the 1994 amount. From here, we scaled the conditional average FLPB amounts to 2007 dollars for the model estimation. For the simulations, FLPB was set equal to the 2012 conditional average scaled up to 2018 dollars.

Estimation

We assume the random shocks follow an extreme value distribution and assume individuals' tastes for active and reserve component service are bivariate normally distributed. Given these distributional assumptions, we can derive choice probabilities for each alternative (active, reserve, civilian) and write an appropriate likelihood equation to estimate the parameters of the model (the parameters of the probability distribution for the shock terms; the population distribution of taste for active component and reserve component service, consisting of the means and standard deviations of active and reserve taste, as well as the correlation between taste for active component service and reserve component service; and switching costs associated with leaving active service for civilian life or entering the reserves from civilian life). The discount factor is assumed to be 0.88, drawing from the estimates from the studies cited at the beginning chapter. The model is estimated by maximum likelihood.[5] The parameters listed in Table 2.3 are estimated by the model.

Table 2.3. Parameter Descriptions

Parameter	Description
τ	Scale parameter of the distribution of the common shock for leaving active duty
λ	Scale parameter of the distribution of the reserve and civilian shock parameters
μ_a	Mean active taste
μ_r	Mean reserve taste
σ_a	Standard deviation of active taste
σ_r	Standard deviation of reserve taste
ρ	Correlation between active and reserve tastes
Switch Cost 1	Switch cost for leaving active before 4 YOS
Switch Cost 2	Switch cost for moving from active to reserve before 4 YOS
Switch Cost 3	Switch cost for moving from active to reserve after at least 4 YOS
Switch Cost 4	Switch cost for moving from civilian to reserve

Discussion of Parameter Estimates

The raw and transformed parameter estimates for each CEA AFSC, excluding RPA Sensor Operators, are shown in Tables 2.4 and 2.5, respectively. Table 2.6 contains the raw and transformed parameter estimates for RPA Sensor Operators. The transformed parameter estimates are in thousands of dollars, except for the correlation of taste parameter.

In most of the models, the mean active taste (μ_a) is negative and statistically significant. The negative estimate indicates that on average mean taste for active duty relative to being a civilian is negative. The transformed switching cost parameter estimates in Table 2.5 and in the last column of Table 2.6 show that the mean taste for active duty ranges from about –\$5,300 for Flight Engineers to –\$57,300 for RPA Sensor Operators. The mean taste for active duty is not estimated to be statistically significant in the Airborne Cryptologist and Special Missions Aviation models. The mean taste for reserve duty relative to being a civilian (μ_r) is also negative and ranges from –\$3,500 for In-Flight Refueling to –\$1,080,100 for Airborne Cryptologists.

[5] Optimization is done using the Broyden-Fletcher-Goldfarb-Shanno (BFGS) algorithm, a standard hill-climbing method. Standard errors of the estimates were computed using numerical differentiation of the likelihood function and taking the square root of the absolute value of the diagonal of the inverse of the Hessian matrix.

The transformed switching cost parameter estimates in Table 2.5 show that the ordering of the switching costs from highest to lowest is broadly consistent across the models, with Airborne Cryptologists being the outlier. In general, the largest cost estimated is the switch from active to reserve before 4 years of active duty service; this is consistent with the service obligation associated with the first term of service. Next in size is the switch from civilian to reserve, and the switch from leaving active duty before 4 years of active service. The cost from switching from active to reserve before 4 years of active duty service ranges from –$67,700 for Special Missions Aviation to –$172,900 Airborne Missions Systems Operators. The smallest cost is the switch from active to reserve after at least 4 YOS, which ranges from –$26,300 for Special Missions Aviation to –$59,700 for Aircraft Loadmasters. Unlike the other CEAs, for Airborne Cryptologists, the ordering of the estimated switching costs from highest to lowest is different. For Airborne Cryptologists, the largest estimated cost is the switch from civilian to reserve (–$720,000) followed by the switch from active to reserve after at least 4 YOS (–$379,700) and the switch from leaving active service before 4 YOS (–$371,900). The switching costs for the RPA Sensor Operator model range from –$111,700 for the cost from switching from active to reserve after 6 years of active duty service to –$634,700 for switching from active to reserve before 4 years of active duty service.

Some of the parameter estimates for the Airborne Cryptologists and RPA Sensor Operators are much larger than those for the other CEAs. For example, the model suggests that Airborne Cryptologists either have a large distaste for being in the reserves, or have great difficulty in finding a suitable reserve position in their preferred geographic area, with a mean reserve taste of almost –$1.1 million and high costs associated with moving from both the active and civilian sectors to the reserves. We can speculate why the parameters are higher for this group (i.e., more career advancement or better compensation in the active component and civilian sector compared to the reserves), but more research is needed to understand why these differences exist.

For the RPA Sensor Operator model, the large parameter estimates may be a result of using a short window of observed data that does not allow us to observe a full active component career profile, or may indeed reflect the larger costs faced by RPA Sensor Operators when making transitions across the active component, reserve component, and civilian sectors relative to other CEAs. Due to the exploratory nature of this model, we suggest that the RPA Sensor Operator DRM model be re-estimated when more years of data are available.

Table 2.4. Parameter Estimates and Standard Errors

	In-Flight Refueling (1A0)		Flight Engineers (1A1)		Aircraft Loadmasters (1A2)		Airborne Missions Systems Operators (1A3)		Airborne Cryptologists (1A8X1)		Special Missions Aviation (1A9)	
	Estimate	Standard Error	Estimate	Standard Error	Estimate	Standard Error	Estimate	Standard Error	Estimate	Standard Error	Estimate	Standard Error
ln(Scale Parameter, τ)	4.01	0.20	3.80	0.12	3.34	0.16	3.73	0.14	–3.88	1712.32	3.71	0.05
ln(Scale Parameter, λ)	2.67	0.36	2.46	0.36	2.90	0.30	2.77	0.27	4.87	0.06	2.17	0.35
–1*ln(Mean Active Taste = μ_a)	2.22	0.20	1.68	0.35	2.55	0.05	2.50	0.07	–5.93	24.68	–13.88	2965.87
–1*ln(Mean Reserve Taste = μ_r)	1.25	0.130	1.76	0.41	1.47	0.32	1.69	0.22	6.98	0.98	1.78	0.12
ln(SD Active Taste = σ_a)	2.54	0.40	–1.82	7.13	2.38	0.18	2.68	0.24	2.20	0.70	–3.32	54.99
ln(SD Reserve Taste =σ_r)	–0.36	2.29	1.51	0.50	1.32	0.60	0.28	0.60	6.61	0.97	–6.58	1531.14
atanh(Taste Correlation = ρ)	1.60	12.49	0.14	0.65	0.20	0.33	–9.73	178.53	0.43	0.02	2.02	2010.51
–1*ln(Switching Cost: Leave Active before completing 4 YOS)	4.29	0.24	N/A	N/A	4.29	0.10	4.60	0.15	5.92	0.12	3.66	0.20
–1*ln(Switching Cost: Switch from Active to Reserve before completing 4 YOS)	4.61	0.36	N/A	N/A	5.02	0.17	5.15	0.16	N/A	N/A	4.21	0.23
–1*ln(Switching Cost: Switch from Active to Reserve after at least 4 YOS)	3.87	0.36	3.63	0.43	4.09	031	3.99	0.30	5.94	0.14	3.27	0.39
1*ln(Switching Cost: Switch from Civilian to Reserve)	4.90	0.26	4.32	0.41	4.86	0.30	4.78	0.15	6.58	0.09	4.95	0.38

SOURCE: Parameter estimates from CEAs entering active duty, 1990–2000.

NOTES: Definitions of variables are provided in Table 2.3. The personal discount factor was assumed to be 0.88 in these models. Coefficients that are not significantly different from zero are grayed out.

Table 2.5. Transformed Parameter Estimates

	In-Flight Refueling (1A0)	Flight Engineers (1A1)	Aircraft Load-masters (1A2)	Airborne Missions Systems Operators (1A3)	Airborne Cryptologists (1A8X1)	Special Missions Aviation (1A9)
Scale Parameter, τ	54.93	44.90	28.33	41.73	0.02	40.73
Scale Parameter, λ	14.48	11.73	18.19	16.01	130.15	8.79
Mean Active Taste = μ_a	−9.24	−5.34	−12.80	−12.22	−0.00	0.00
Mean Reserve Taste = μ_r	−3.48	−5.83	−4.37	−5.44	−1080.09	−5.90
SD Active Taste = σ_a	12.72	0.16	10.80	14.58	9.00	0.04
SD Reserve Taste = σ_r	1.44	4.52	3.73	1.32	740.61	0.00
Taste Correlation = ρ	0.92	0.14	0.20	−1.00	0.41	0.97
Switch Cost: Leave Active Before 4 YOS	−72.72	N/A	−72.66	−99.57	−371.94	−38.93
Switch Cost: Switch from Active to Reserve before 4 YOS	−134.62	N/A	−151.51	−172.92	N/A	−67.67
Switch Cost: Switch from Active to Reserve after at least 4 YOS	−48.12	−37.77	−59.73	−54.16	−379.71	−26.25
Switch Cost: Switch from Civilian to Reserve	−100.95	−75.35	−128.38	−118.68	−719.97	−52.04

NOTE: Transformed parameters are denominated in thousands of dollars, with the exception of the taste correlation. Definitions of variables are provided in Table 2.3. Coefficients that are not significantly different from zero are grayed out.

Table 2.6. Parameter Estimates, RPA Sensor Operators

	Parameter Estimate	Standard Error	Transformed Parameter
Scale Parameter, τ	5.06	1.04	153.54
Scale Parameter, λ	3.53	0.32	34.00
Mean Active Taste = μ_a	4.02	0.79	−57.34
Mean Reserve Taste = μ_r	−5.18	89.51	−0.00
SD Active Taste = σ_a	−1.16	37.72	0.44
SD Reserve Taste = σ_r	−3.21	495.50	0.03
Taste Correlation = ρ	−1.82	583.38	1.00
Switch Cost: Leave Active Before 4 YOS	6.16	1.02	−475.10
Switch Cost: Leave Active After 4 YOS and Before 6 YOS	5.45	1.02	−232.88
Switch Cost: Switch from Active to Reserve Before 4 YOS	6.45	0.81	−634.70
Switch Cost: Switch from Active to Reserve After 4 YOS and Before 6 YOS	5.84	0.75	−343.09
Switch Cost: Switch from Active to Reserve After 6 YOS	4.72	0.27	−111.70
Switch Cost: Switch from Civilian to Reserve	5.44	0.31	−230.56

SOURCE: Parameter estimates from CEAs entering active duty, 2009–2013.
NOTES: Definitions of variables are provided in Table 2.3. The personal discount factor was assumed to be 0.88 in these models. Transformed parameters are denominated in thousands of dollars, with the exception of the taste correlation. Coefficients that are not significantly different from zero are grayed out.

Model Fits

The models fit the data well. Figures 2.1 through 2.7 show for each CEA AFSC the predicted active retention (red line) and the Kaplan-Meier survival curves for the observed data (black line). The Kaplan-Meier curve is produced using a non-parametric method to estimate a survival function from lifetime data.[6] The Kaplan-Meier 95 percent confidence intervals are shown in dashed lines.[7] In general, the predicted and observed lines are close together and within the confidence intervals. We calculate each model's pseudo R-squared to measure its goodness of fit. Pseudo R-squared tends to be lower in value than ordinary R-squared (as is used in linear regression). Daniel McFadden (1977) described values from 0.2 to 0.4 as showing "excellent fit." The pseudo R-squared values range from 0.66 to 0.84 indicating that the models fit the data well.[8]

---

[6] For more details see Kaplan and Meier (1958).

[7] The bottom of each figure shows the model estimates and can be ignored by the reader. They are included to ensure we can track the estimates associated with each figure.

[8] We note that the models under predict the drop in retention at years of service four for Aircraft Loadmasters, Airborne Mission Systems Operators, and Airborne Cryptologists (Figures 2.3, 2.4, and 2.5, respectively). We suspect that the models have trouble producing portions of the retention profile that experience large changes in slope. In the case of Aircraft Loadmasters and Airborne Mission Systems Operators, there is a large change in slope when moving from the large negative slope between three and four years of service to the flatter negative slope at five years of service and beyond). We further note that the exploratory RPA Sensor Operator model prediction is noticeably higher than the Kaplan-Meier curve in Figure 2.7 for years 6 through 9.

Figure 2.1. In-Flight Refueling (1A0) Model Fit

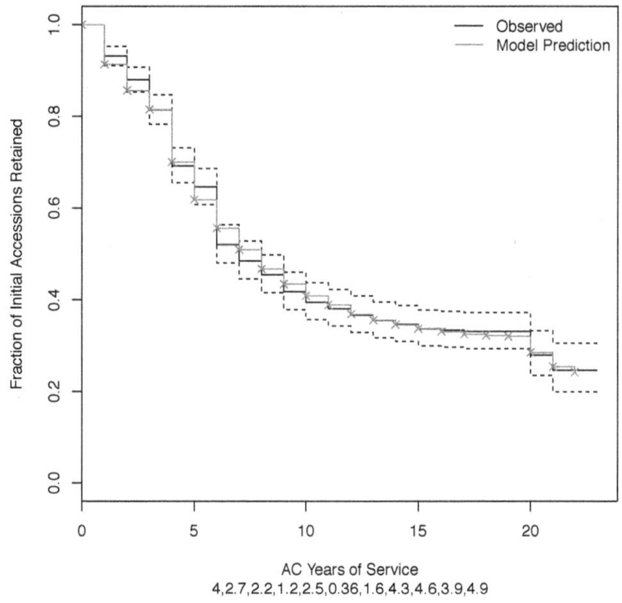

SOURCE: Authors' computations.

Figure 2.2. Flight Engineers (1A1) Model Fit

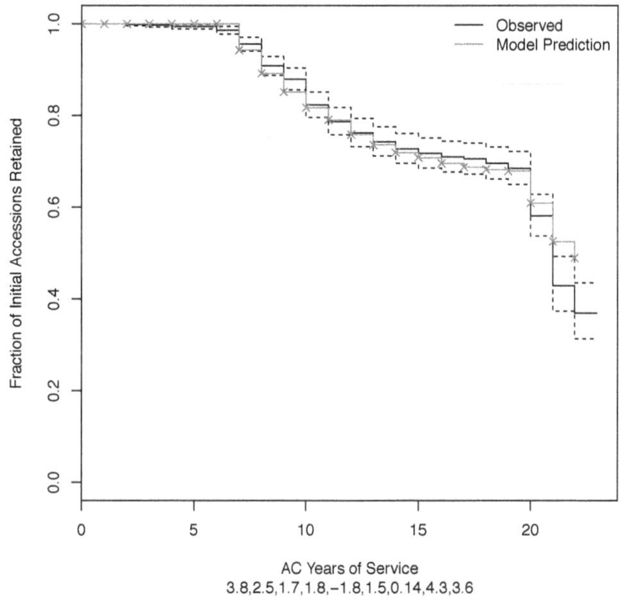

SOURCE: Authors' computations.

Figure 2.3. Aircraft Loadmasters (1A2) Model Fit

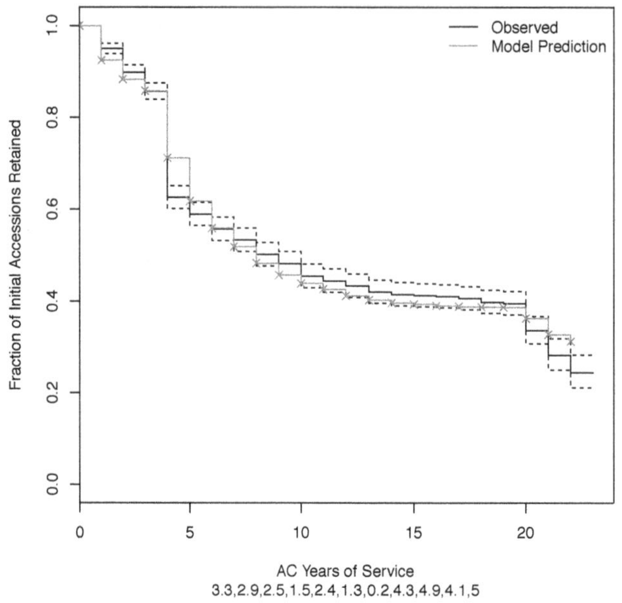

SOURCE: Authors' computations.

Figure 2.4. Airborne Mission Systems Operators (1A3) Model Fit

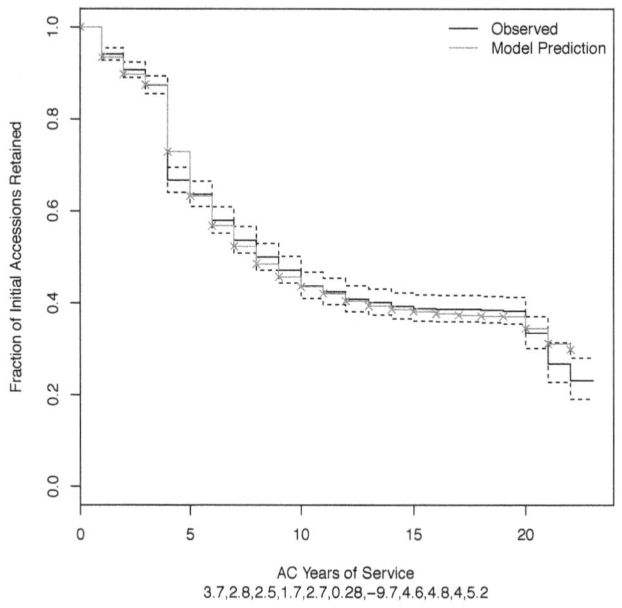

SOURCE: Authors' computations.

Figure 2.5 Airborne Cryptologists (1A8X1) Model Fit

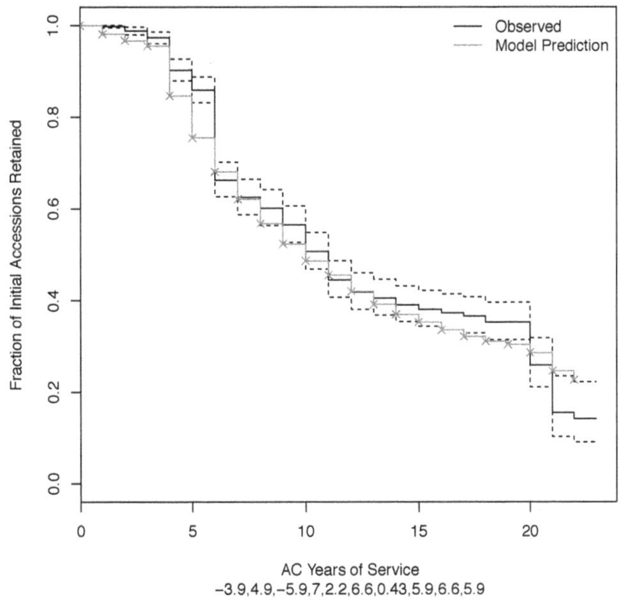

SOURCE: Authors' computations.

Figure 2.6. Special Missions Aviation (1A9) Model Fit

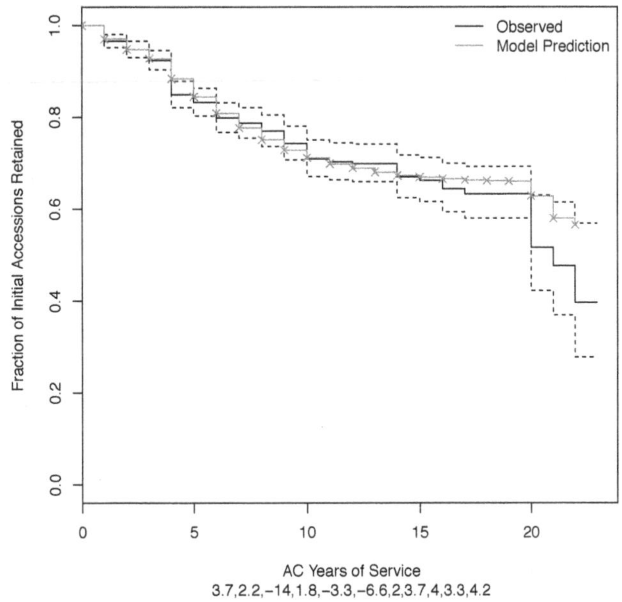

SOURCE: Authors' computations.

Figure 2.7. RPA Sensor Operators (1U0) Model Fit

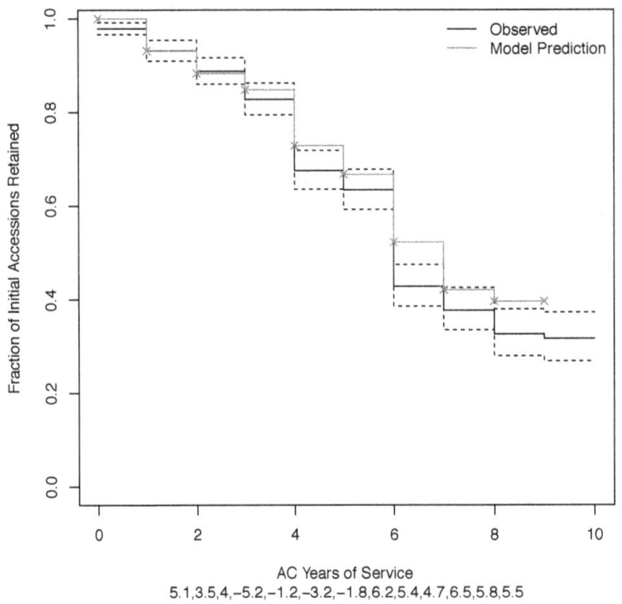

SOURCE: Authors' computations.

Simulation Capability

We also developed simulation code that allowed us to simulate retention over a CEA career in the active and reserve components and to compute the cumulative retention profile in the steady state under alternative S&I policies. We can then use the simulated retention profile to compute personnel costs. These simulations provide a capability to determine the most cost-effective S&I policy to achieve a given force size and retention profile for a particular CEA specialty.

To demonstrate the simulation capability, we show in this subsection the simulated effects of changing CSIP and SRBs on CEA retention and per capita cost. Costs include regular military compensation (i.e., basic pay, allowances, and the federal income tax advantage for allowances), CSIP, SRBs, and the blended retirement system (BRS). BRS costs include the retirement accrual charge associated with the defined benefit plan portion of BRS, continuation pay costs, and the Air Force contributions to the Thrift Savings Plan. The retirement accrual cost is the normal cost percentage (NCP)[9] times the basic pay bill of the force, where we assumed that the NCP for active duty personnel is 30.4 percent (U.S. Department of Defense [DoD], Office of the Actuary, 2019). We assume that continuation pay is equal to 2.5 times basic pay at 12 YOS, and we

---

[9] The Air Force contributes the accrual charge to the Military Retirement Fund to help fund the future retirement liability associated with its current force. The NCP is the percentage of basic pay that must be contributed over the entire active career of a typical group of new entrants to pay for future retirement and survivor benefits for that group and is calculated by the U.S. Department of Defense (DoD) Office of the Actuary.

assume that the Air Force would contribute 4 percent of basic pay on behalf of each member at each year of service.

For this exercise, recruiting and training costs are not included in the per capita cost estimate. Recruiting and training costs will be discussed and incorporated into the analysis in Chapter 3. To compute per capita cost, we divide total cost by the total force size for the CEA occupation. Per capita costs will change not only because of a change in S&I pay but also because the experience mix of the force might change, thereby changing pay and retirement accrual costs. For example, if S&I pay increases retention and increases the experience mix of the force, per capita costs will increase because more experienced personnel receive higher military pay and are more likely to reach 20 YOS, so the retirement accrual charge will increase. For each S&I pay simulation, we compare the simulated retention and per capita cost to those for a baseline case with the CSIP rates listed in Table 2.1 and with SRB multipliers as of July 31, 2019 (Table 2.7).

Table 2.7. Selective Reenlistment Bonus Multipliers, Effective July 31, 2019

	Zone A	Zone B	Zone C
In-Flight Refueling (1A0)	3	3	2
Flight Engineers (1A1)	3	0	0
Aircraft Loadmasters (1A2)	3	3	0
Airborne Mission Systems Operators (1A3)	0	0	0
Airborne Cryptologists (1A8X1)	6	5	3.5
Special Missions Aviation (1A9)	3	3	2

SOURCE: Air Force Personnel Center, 2019.

We consider six S&I policies: three that expand CSIP and three that expand SRBs. First, we simulate the retention effects from increasing CSIP to $1,000 per month, which is the statutory maximum, for those with less than 10 YOS. Second, we increase CSIP to $1,000 per month for all YOS. Third, we replace CSIP with the maximum officer Aviation Incentive Pay (AvIP) monthly rate, which is the officer equivalent of CSIP. Instead of strictly increasing with YAS like CSIP, AvIP increases until 14 YAS and then decreases after that. With the exception of service members with 2 or fewer YAS or those with over 24 YAS, maximum AvIP is more generous than CSIP (Table 2.8). Given the sponsor's interest in promoting retention among CEAs with less experience, we conduct simulations that vary SRB Zone A and Zone B. For the three policy simulations with expanded SRBs, we increased both the SRB Zone A and B multipliers to six, seven, and eight, respectively.

Table 2.8. Critical Skills Incentive Pay Versus Maximum Aviation Incentive Pay

Years of Aviation Service	CSIP	AVIP
2 or less	$225	$150
Over 2	$225	$250
Over 4	$350	$250
Over 6	$350	$800
Over 8	$500	$800
Over 10	$500	$1,000
Over 14	$600	$1,000
Over 22	$600	$700
Over 24	$600	$450

SOURCE: Office of the Under Secretary of Defense (Comptroller), 2018, Chapter 22.

For illustrative purposes, we present simulation results for In-Flight Refueling (1A0) in this chapter. Summary tables showing the effects of the different policies on retention and per capita cost for the other CEA AFSCs are reported in Appendix C. We present the percentage increase in overall retention and retention among those with less than 10 YOS specifically to show the impact on CEAs with different experience.

Table 2.9 shows that, as expected, retention is expected to increase under all six cases, though the percentage increase varies across the cases. Retention also increases among those with fewer than 10 YOS in all six cases. However, the cost-effectiveness of these policies in increasing retention is not the same. We find that expanding the SRB multiplier is generally a more cost-effective means of increasing retention than expanding CSIP. This is because, unlike SRBs, CSIP does not require a service obligation. Service members can receive CSIP and leave. The service obligation required for receipt of SRBs induces a stronger retention incentive for a given dollar spent than does a policy that increases CSIP. For example, for In-Flight Refueling, the percentage increase in per capita costs is higher under the three simulations that increase CSIP than the percentage increase in per capita costs under the three simulations that increase SRBs. The exception is the case where the percentage increase in per capita cost is roughly the same when CSIP is increased to $1,000 for those with less than 10 YOS and when SRB Zone A and B multipliers are increased to seven (both 5.2 percent increase in per capita cost). The conclusion that increasing SRBs is more cost-effective than increasing CSIP to achieve a more experienced force holds for the other CEA specialties, as well (see Appendix C). We find that expanding SRBs yields greater increases in retention compared with the increases from expanding CSIP for a comparable increase in per capita cost, with the magnitude of the difference varying by CEA AFSC. We also find that to achieve similar increases in retention, expanding CSIP is more expensive than expanding SRBs. To further demonstrate that increasing SRBs is more cost-effective than increasing CSIP, we compute the SRB multipliers that would yield a similar percentage increase in retention for those with less than 10 YOS when CSIP is increased to $1,000 for those with less than 10 YOS and compare costs.[10] Table 2.10 shows that the SRB policy that most closely matches the increase in retention for those with less than 10 YOS not only costs less, but also yields higher retention overall when compared with increasing CSIP generosity.

Table 2.9. Simulations with Different Special and Incentive Pays, In-Flight Refueling (1A0)

	% Increase in Retention	% Increase in Retention, Less than 10 YOS	% Increase in Per Capita Cost
$1,000 CSIP at < 10 YOS	10.8	9.0	5.2
Replace CSIP with AvIP	16.2	6.3	7.0
$1,000 CSIP at all YOS	27.8	12.6	12.9
SRB Zone A & B Multipliers = 6	12.7	7.7	4.0
SRB Zone A & B Multipliers = 7	16.5	10.1	5.2
SRB Zone A & B Multipliers = 8	19.8	12.2	6.3

SOURCE: Authors' computations.
NOTES: Percentage changes are relative to a baseline with CSIP rates as of October 1, 2017, and SRB multipliers as of July 31, 2019.

Table 2.10. Comparing Cost-Effectiveness of Increasing Critical Skills Incentive Pay Versus Increasing Selective Reenlistment Bonuses

	$1,000 CSIP at YOS <10			SRB Policy			
	% Increase in Retention	% Increase in Retention, Less Than 10 YOS	% Increase in Per Capita Cost	SRB Multipliers A and B	% Increase in Retention	% Increase in Retention, Less Than 10 YOS	% Increase in Per Capita Cost
In-Flight Refueling	10.8	9.0	5.2	6.5	14.7	8.9	4.6
Flight Engineers	2.3	0.7	4.5	3.5	9.9	1.8	4.3
Aircraft Loadmasters	11.4	10.4	4.6	6.5	15.5	10.4	4.0
Airborne Mission Systems Operators	12.8	10.7	5.9	3.5	19.6	10.8	5.4
Airborne Cryptologists	6.7	3.8	6.1	9	8.8	4.0	5.0
Special Missions Aviation	2.3	1.7	3.4	6.5	2.8	1.7	2.8

SOURCE: Authors' computations.
NOTES: Percentage changes are relative to a baseline with CSIP rates as of October 1, 2017, and SRB multipliers as of July 31, 2019.

[10] SRB multipliers are set at whole or half integer amounts. As a consequence, it is not necessarily possible to find an SRB policy to exactly match the growth in retention for those with less than 10 YOS under the CSIP policy.

Summary

In this chapter, we first provided an overview of the DRM and described the data used for the models. Next, we discussed the parameter estimates and showed that the models generally fit the data well. To demonstrate the simulation capability of the models, we estimated the changes in retention and per capita costs from increasing the generosity of CSIP and SRBs using six different policy scenarios. In addition, we compared the per capita costs between increasing CSIP and increasing SRBs while holding retention of personnel with under 10 YOS roughly constant and found that increasing SRBs is more cost-effective. This result is due to SRBs being associated with a service obligation, unlike CSIP, which service members can receive and subsequently leave.

3. Retaining Career Enlisted Aviators Versus Expanding the Training Pipeline

One goal of this study was to show the trade-off between retaining CEAs by expanding S&I pays and expanding the training pipeline but incurring recruiting and training costs. Increasing S&I pays and expanding accessions have different implications for the experience mix of the CEA population and cost. In this chapter, we first provide a conceptual framework for these costs and benefits and describe the data used on recruiting and training costs. Because we find that SRBs are more cost-effective than CSIP at retaining CEAs, we focus on SRBs and conduct a series of simulations for each CEA that varies SRB generosity. With these simulations, we

1. graphically show how steady state per capita costs change with SRB generosity when we use the existing recruiting and training cost data
2. estimate how the experience mix changes with SRB generosity to determine whether optimal percentages of junior and more senior personnel are met
3. calculate how high recruiting and training costs would have to be to make retaining experienced CEAs through SRBs more cost-effective than increasing accessions. We call these thresholds tipping points.

We provide a summary at the end of the chapter.

Conceptual Framework

We demonstrate our conceptual framework in Figure 3.1, which shows the simulated steady-state retention profile for In-Flight Refueling (1A0) under two cases, holding force size constant at 792 enlisted personnel.[11] In one case, the SRB multipliers for Zones A and B are set equal to 3. In the other case, the SRB multipliers for Zones A and B are set equal to 9. Increasing SRBs increases the proportion of the force that are experienced CEAs. As shown in Figure 3.1, accessions are lower when SRBs are higher and the experience mix of the force increases. In particular, steady-state accessions are 35 versus 42 when SRBs are higher in the figure and the percentage of force with 10 or more YOS is 6.9 percent higher. The question we seek to answer is whether per capita costs are greater under scenarios such as the first case (lower S&I pays but higher accessions) or under scenarios such as the second case (higher S&I pays but fewer accessions).

[11] We chose 792 because it is the estimated size of the 1A0 population as of March 2019 using the DMDC WEX data.

Figure 3.1. Simulated Steady-State Inflight Refueling (1A0) Retention Profile, Selective Reenlistment Bonus Multipliers A and B Equal 3 Versus 9

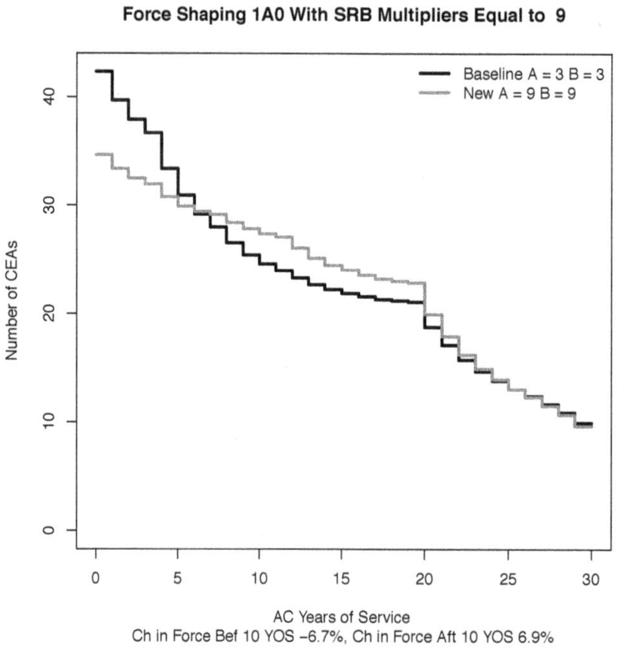

SOURCE: Authors' computations.

Holding force size constant, the per capita cost of a CEA is given by the following formula:

$$C=\frac{[\text{Personnel cost}+(\text{Recruiting and Training cost per CEA*Number of CEAs trained})]}{\text{CEA force size}}$$

Personnel costs for the CEAs include the cost of RMC, S&I pays, and costs associated with the BRS. Recruiting and training cost per CEA is multiplied by the number of CEAs accessed and trained to calculate the total recruiting and training cost.

The conceptual framework implied by this formula is summarized in Figure 3.2. To hold force size constant, either SRBs are lower and accessions are higher (the upper left quadrant in the figure) or SRBs are higher and accessions are lower (the lower right quadrant). Otherwise, the force size increases (upper right quadrant) or the force size decreases (lower left quadrant).

Figure 3.2. Conceptual Framework

	Lower SRB	Higher SRB
More Accessions	Less experienced force Lower pay and SRB bill Higher recruiting and training costs (assuming force size is constant)	N/A (larger force size)
Fewer Accessions	N/A (smaller force size)	More experienced force Higher pay and SRB bill Lower recruiting and training costs (assuming force size is constant)

Maintaining the CEA force size when SRBs are lower and accessions are higher yields a less experienced force, as shown in Figure 3.1. A less experienced force is less costly in terms of cost of basic pay, since basic pay increases with years of experience. Retirement accrual costs and employer contributions to the Thrift Savings Plan are also lower for a less experienced force because the basic pay bill is lower. On the other hand, more accessions cause the total cost of training CEAs to increase. Although not included in our trade-off estimates, we note that there may be capacity constraints that currently limit the number of new recruits who could be trained as CEAs. Expanding training capacity would require additional costs.

Maintaining the CEA force size when SRBs are higher and accessions are lower causes the force to be more experienced, as shown in Figure 3.1. Fewer accessions mean that recruiting and training costs are lower, and because a given accession stays longer when SRBs are higher, the Air Force gets a greater return on investment from each new recruit. However, a more experienced force means that compensation and retirement related costs are higher.

The conceptual framework depicted in Figure 3.2 demonstrates that the direction of the overall change in total cost—that is, recruiting, training and personnel costs—is unclear when force size is held constant. As a result, we use the CEA specific models to calculate simulated per capita costs, including both training and personnel costs, for different sizes of SRBs to estimate the trade-off between retaining CEAs and training new CEAs.

Recruiting and Training Cost Data

We use recruiting and training cost data from AFI 65-503, Table A18-1 and Table A35-1, which report variable costs by enlisted Air Force occupation. The cost estimates reported in Tables A18-1 and A35-1 come from Air Education Training Command. Table A18-1 includes costs from acquisition through initial specialty training, including[12]

[12] AFSCs with no technical training requirements include only accession and basic military training costs.

- cost per graduate for training courses required for specific AFSCs at the basic skill level
- acquisition costs, including
  - costs of recruiting, initial travel and initial clothing issued
  - cost of basic training at the Air Force Military Training Center
- student pay and allowances
- time in transit and waiting for class to begin.

Table A35-1 reports the variable training costs for representative aircrew enlisted personnel (i.e., flight training costs) for In-Flight Refueling, Flight Engineers, and Aircraft Loadmasters by type of aircraft. The cost from flying for the other CEAs (Airborne Missions Systems Operators, Airborne Cryptologists, and Special Missions Aviation) are assumed to be borne by pilots. However, if flight training costs should be shared with these CEAs, then the training costs estimates used in this exercise underestimate the true costs.

Because the most recent recruiting and training cost data available are for fiscal year 2014, we inflate these figures to 2018 dollars for the analysis.[13] Table 3.1 shows fiscal year 2014 costs for each CEA and the inflated 2018 estimated costs.

Table 3.1. Estimated Recruiting and Training Costs, by Career Enlisted Aviator Occupation

Career Enlisted Aviator	AFI 65-503, Table 18-1a, Fiscal Year 2014	AFI 65-503, Table 35-1, Fiscal Year 2014	Total Estimated 2018
In-Flight Refueling (1A0)	$36,929	$232,352	$289,805
Flight Engineers (1A1)	$58,114	$175,652 (C-130H) to $1,390,480 (CV-22)	$251,583 (C-130H) to $1,559,003 (CV-22)
Aircraft Loadmasters (1A2)	$39,008	$66,633 (C-130J) to $254,893 (C-17)	$113,692 (C-130J) to $316,301 (C-17)
Airborne Mission Systems Operators (1A3)	$44,567	N/A	$47,964
Airborne Cryptologists (1A8X1)	$79,735 (Spanish) to $180,283 (Arabic)	N/A	$85,812 (Spanish) to $194,024 (Arabic)
Special Missions Aviation (1A9)	$33,824	N/A	$36,402
RPA Sensor Operators (1U0)	$36,732	N/A	$39,532

Simulations of How Steady-State Per Capita Costs Vary with Selective Reenlistment Bonuses

To estimate the trade-off between retaining CEAs versus increasing accessions, we use the models described in Chapter 2 to conduct simulations in which we vary the SRB Zone A and B multipliers from zero to 15 holding force size constant. The force size for each CEA is based on

[13] To inflate the fiscal year 2014 costs to 2018 values, we use the CPI-U values for October 2013 and the annual value for 2018.

March 2019 DMDC WEX data. For each simulation, we estimate the per capita cost in 2018 dollars inclusive of the estimated recruiting and training costs listed in Table 3.1.

Figures 3.3 through 3.8 show how the per capita cost (in 2018 dollars) changes as the SRB multipliers vary. For example, in Figure 3.3, with no SRB, the per capita cost of a 1A0 is just below $120,000. With an SRB multiplier of 15, the per capita cost increases to a little over $130,000. We find that in every case but one (Flight Engineers), per capita costs increase with the SRB multipliers. The implication is that, in general, to sustain a given CEA force size, increasing SRBs is less efficient than increasing accessions. Although increasing SRBs leads to a more experienced and expensive force, reductions in recruiting and training costs do not offset these costs. An important caveat, also noted above, is that these per capita costs do not include the costs associated with increasing absorption of additional junior personnel or training capacity constraints, including the cost of additional instructors.

As mentioned, the exception is Flight Engineers for the CV-22 (Figure 3.4). For this AFSC, the per capita cost decreases when SRB multipliers range from 0 to 2.5 and increases when SRB multipliers range from 2.5 to 15, assuming the maximum recruiting and training costs (i.e., those being trained to work on CV-22 aircraft). Since 2001, the SRB Zone A and B multipliers for Flight Engineers have ranged from 1 to 3 when Flight Engineers have been eligible for SRBs. Based on this historical range, our analysis suggests that for Flight Engineers who are training to be part of the flight crew on CV-22 aircraft, retaining more-experienced personnel using SRBs is more efficient than increasing accessions to sustain a force size when SRB multipliers are less than 2.5, and increasing accessions is more efficient if SRB multipliers are above 2.5.

Figure 3.3. Cost Per In-Flight Refueling (1A0), by SRB A and B Multiplier

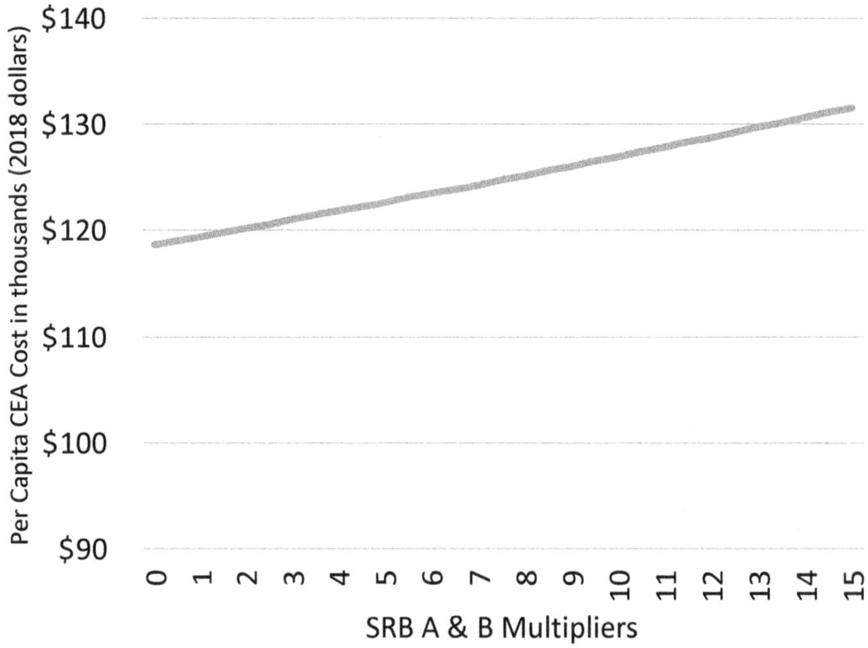

SOURCE: Authors' computations.
NOTES: Forecasted 2018 per capita training costs = $290,000.

Figure 3.4. Cost Per Flight Engineer (1A1), by SRB A and B Multiplier

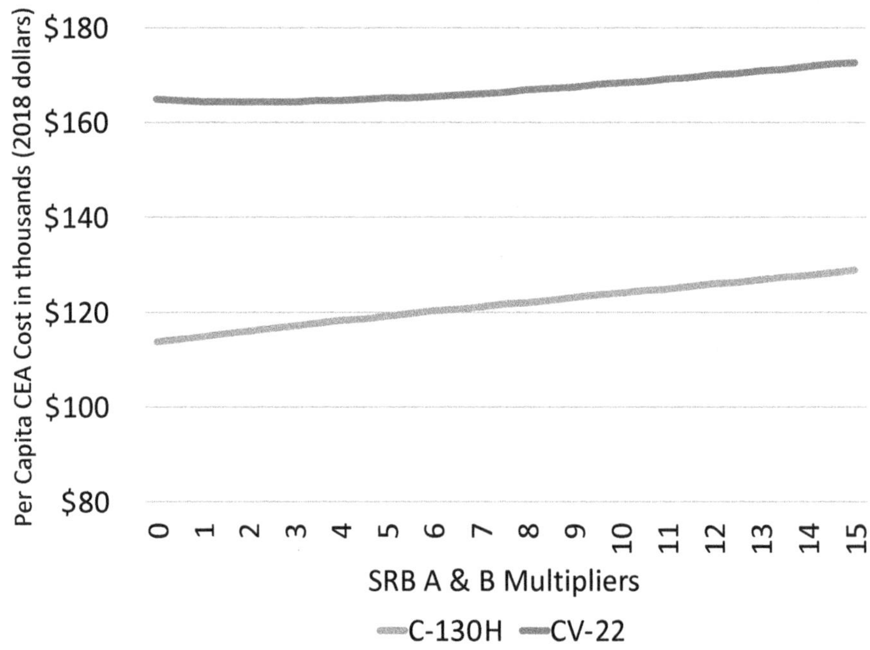

SOURCE: Authors' computations.
NOTES: Forecasted 2018 per capita training Costs = $252,000 (C-130H), $1,559,000 (CV-22).

Figure 3.5. Cost Per Aircraft Loadmaster (1A2), by SRB A and B Multiplier

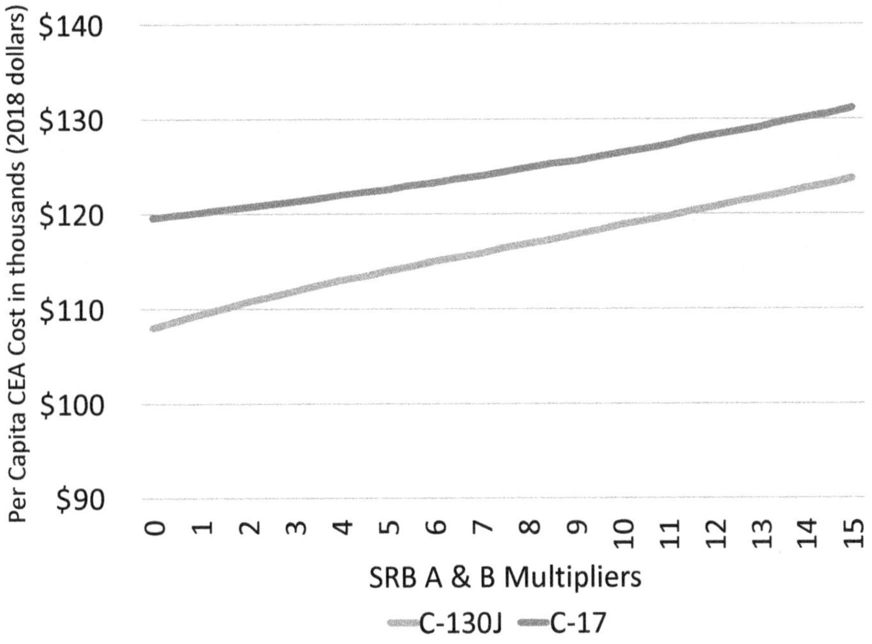

SOURCE: Authors' computations.
NOTES: Forecasted 2018 per capita training costs = $114,000 (C-130J), $316,000 (C-17).

Figure 3.6. Cost Per Airborne Mission Systems Operator (1A3), by A and B Multiplier

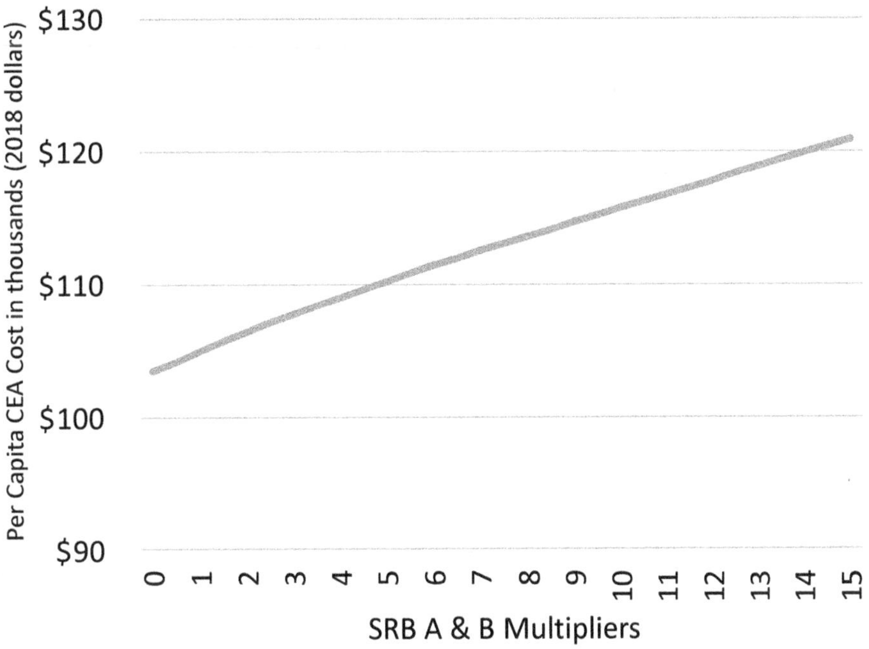

SOURCE: Authors' computations.
NOTES: Forecasted 2018 per capita training costs = $48,000.

Figure 3.7. Cost Per Airborne Cryptologist (1A8X1), by SRB A and B Multiplier

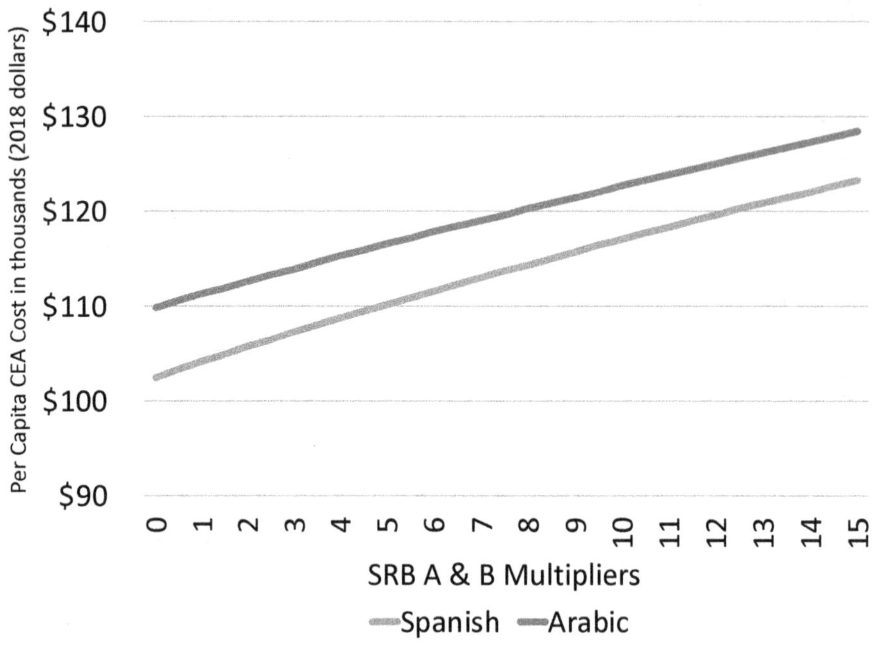

SOURCE: Authors' computations.
NOTES: Forecasted 2018 per capita training costs = $86,000 for Spanish and $194,000 for Arabic.

Figure 3.8. Cost Per Special Missions Aviation (1A9) by SRB A and B Multiplier

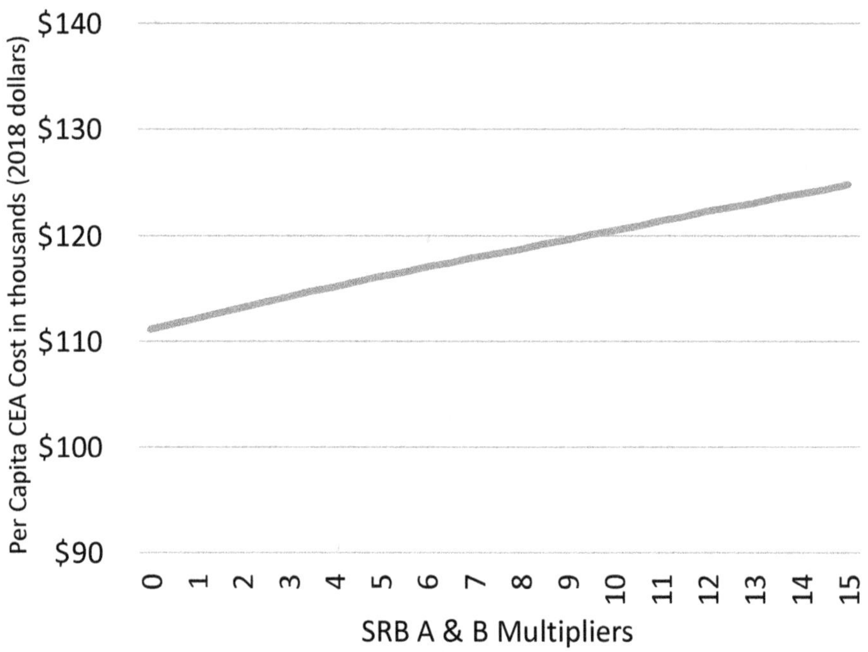

SOURCE: Authors' computations.
NOTES: Forecasted 2018 per capita training costs = $36,000.

Our main finding—that increasing accessions is more efficient than retaining experienced personnel by increasing SRBs—is driven by the high cost of experienced CEA personnel relative to the low cost of recruiting and training new personnel. This result is in contrast with the results for pilots. In Mattock et al. (2019), we found that it is more efficient to retain pilots with higher aviator bonuses than to access and train additional pilots. Per pilot training costs are as high as $10.9 million for an F-22 pilot, so increasing bonuses were always more efficient. In this study, per CEA training costs are low enough that increasing accessions is more efficient than retaining more-experienced personnel through larger SRBs. However, accessing CEAs rather than retaining them may result in a force experience mix that is too junior. A force that is too junior could mean that there is an inadequate number of experienced personnel to serve as instructors and evaluators.

How Experience Mix Changes with Selective Reenlistment Bonus Generosity

Although incorporating the cost of increasing training capacity is beyond the scope of this report, we further explored whether the force size would be too junior, or, put differently, would deviate from the Air Force's desired experience mix under policies that emphasized accessions over increasing retention through higher S&I pays. According to feedback from the sponsor, the desired force mix would have at least 35 percent of the force with enough experience to serve as instructors and evaluators who train junior personnel. In general, instructors and evaluators would be in the Staff Sergeant, Technical Sergeant, and Senior Master Sergeant ranks. For our analysis, we used YOS as a proxy for the potential pool of CEAs who could be instructors and evaluators. With the exception of Flight Engineers, we assume that personnel with 4 to 15 YOS could serve as instructors and evaluators. For Flight Engineers, we assume that personnel with 8 to 17 YOS could serve as instructors and evaluators.

Table 3.2 shows the percentage of the force eligible to be instructors and evaluators under two scenarios: when the SRB Zone A and B multipliers are set equal to 0 and when they are set to 15. The first scenario results in the highest number of accessions to sustain a given force size, and the second results in the fewest. Consequently, we would expect the first scenario to be the most likely to fail to achieve the Air Force 35 percent threshold for a desired experience mix. We find that across all the CEAs, the 35 percent threshold is met under both policy scenarios. That is, even under the scenario in which accessions are greatest (SRB A and B multipliers are 0), at least 35 percent of each CEA inventory is sufficiently experienced to be an instructor or evaluator. These results suggest that the binding constraint to determining whether it is more cost effective to train new recruits or retain more experienced personnel through SRBs is recruiting and training costs and not achieving the 35 percent threshold.

Table 3.2. Percentage of Personnel Eligible to be Instructors and Evaluators, by Career Enlisted Aviator Occupation and Selective Reenlistment Bonus

Career Enlisted Aviator	SRB A and B Multipliers = 0	SRB A and B Multipliers = 15
In-Flight Refueling (1A0)	43.3	48.7
Flight Engineers (1A1)	35.4	37.6
Aircraft Loadmasters (1A2)	41.2	47.9
Airborne Missions Systems Operators (1A3)	41.7	48.5
Airborne Cryptologists (1A8X1)	48.3	51.1
Special Missions Aviation (1A9)	42.2	42.5

SOURCE: Authors' computations.
NOTES: For In-Flight Refueling, Aircraft Loadmasters, Airborne Missions Systems Operators, Airborne Cryptologists, and Special Missions Aviation, personnel are assumed to be eligible to be instructors and evaluators if they have 4 to 15 YOS. Flight engineers are assumed to be eligible to be instructors and evaluators if they have 8 to 17 YOS.

Identifying Recruiting and Training Cost Tipping Points

In this section, we calculate tipping points for each CEA AFSC's recruiting and training cost, assuming that force size is held constant. The tipping point identifies the value of recruiting and training costs such that retaining CEAs using SRBs is more cost-effective than increasing accessions. For recruiting and training costs below the tipping point, it is more cost-effective to train new recruits to become CEAs compared with retaining more-experienced CEAs using SRBs. And the opposite is the case for recruiting and training costs above the tipping point.

Calculation of the tipping points is useful because the recruiting and training costs used in the prior section are estimates, and estimation error could cause these to misrepresent the true costs of accessing new CEAs. Furthermore, future recruiting and training costs could be different from those previously estimated.

To calculate the tipping points, we first identified the historical range of SRB Zone A and B multipliers for each CEA AFSC from 2001 onward using SRB multiplier data compiled in Appendix B of Tong et al. (2020).[14] For simplicity, we use the lowest and highest multipliers across both Zone A and Zone B to identify the range of both multipliers for the calculation of tipping points. To identify the tipping point, we first assumed recruiting and training costs were $5,000. We then calculated the per capita cost for that AFSC over the range of SRB multipliers listed in in Table 3.2. If the per capita cost over that SRB range was constant or strictly decreasing, this was the tipping point—that is, SRB costs give the same or lower per capita cost than recruiting and training costs. If not, we increased recruiting and training costs in $5,000 increments until the per capita cost over the SRB range was constant or strictly decreasing and set the tipping point equal to that recruiting and training cost. Note that we increased recruiting

[14] Historical data compiled for Tong et al. (2020) do not include Special Missions Aviation. As of July 31, 2019, the SRB zones A and B multipliers for Special Missions Aviation was 3. To calculate the tipping point for this AFSC, we used a range of 2 to 4 for the SRB A and B multipliers.

and training costs in $5,000 increments up to $1.5 million, which is the maximum recruiting and training cost reported among the CEAs in Table 3.1.

Table 3.3 lists the tipping points calculated for each CEA along with the range of SRB Zone A and B multipliers used for this exercise. These tipping points range (in 2018 dollars) from $580,000 for Aircraft Loadmasters to $1,500,000 for Special Missions Aviation. Comparing these tipping point estimates to the estimated training costs shown in the final column of Table 3.1 indicates that, with the exception of CV-22 Flight Engineers, training and accession costs would need to increase substantially before it would be more cost-effective to retain rather than recruit CEAs. For CV-22 Flight Engineers, estimated recruiting and training costs and the estimated tipping point are approximately the same, implying that that increasing SRBs and increasing accessions to sustain a given force size could yield a similar cost.

Table 3.3. Estimated Training Cost Tipping Points, by Career Enlisted Aviator Occupation

Career Enlisted Aviator	Range of SRB A and B Multipliers	Tipping Point (in 2018 dollars)
In-Flight Refueling (1A0)	0.5 to 3	$585,000
Flight Engineers (1A1)	1 to 3	$1,485,000
Aircraft Loadmasters (1A2)	1 to 4.5	$580,000
Airborne Mission Systems Operators (1A3)	1 to 4.5	$720,000
Airborne Cryptologists (1A8X1)	3 to 7	$1,015,000
Special Missions Aviation (1A9)	2 to 4	$1,500,000

NOTES: At training costs above the tipping points, it would be more cost-effective to retain CEAs rather than to increase accessions, assuming that SRB Zone A and B multipliers are within the listed range. At training costs below the tipping points, it would be more cost-effective to increase accessions rather than retain CEAs, assuming that SRB Zone A and B multipliers are within the listed range.

Summary

In this chapter, we described a conceptual framework demonstrating why cost-effectiveness from retaining more CEAs using SRBs versus increasing accessions is theoretically ambiguous for a given force size. This framework motivates the need to empirically estimate this trade-off. To do so, we conducted simulations that vary SRB generosity using the CEA AFSC–specific models described in Chapter 2 and incorporated existing recruiting and training cost data to estimate per capita costs.

We first find that, with the exception of CV-22 Flight Engineers, increasing accessions is more cost-effective than retaining more experienced CEAs with SRBs because per capita costs strictly increase with SRB generosity. For Flight Engineers, the high cost of recruiting and training to be part of flight crew on CV-22 aircraft makes retaining experienced personnel through SRBs efficient when SRB multipliers are below 2.5. When SRB multipliers are above 2.5, it is more efficient to increase accessions to sustain CV-22 Flight Engineer force size.

Second, based on experience-mix benchmarks provided by the sponsor, we determine that changing SRB generosity would allow the each of the CEA AFSC workforces to maintain optimal percentages of instructors and evaluators that ensure that enough staffing is available to train junior personnel. As a result, the binding constraint to determining whether it is more cost-effective to train new recruits or retain more-experienced personnel through SRBs is recruiting and training costs and not achieving the desired experience-mix.

Finally, we estimated how high recruiting and training costs would need to make it more cost-effective to retain experienced personnel through SRBs rather than increasing accessions. These tipping-point calculations demonstrate that, with the exception of Flight Engineers of CV-22 aircraft, recruiting and training costs would have to increase substantially before retaining experienced personnel with SRBs becomes more cost-effective than increasing accessions. For CV-22 Flight Engineers, estimated recruiting and training costs are sufficiently close to the AFSC's estimated tipping point that increasing SRBs and increasing accessions to sustain a given force size cost could be considered approximately the same. This finding suggests that the Air Force could be indifferent between the two options from a cost standpoint.

4. Concluding Thoughts

In this report, we developed and estimated dynamic retention models by CEA specialty. These estimated models allow us to simulate how CEA retention behavior changes in response to changes in S&I pays. They also allow us to develop the analytic capability to determine the efficient amount of these pays, given that an alternative policy would be to sustain a given force size through recruiting and retaining new CEAs.

Our first key conclusion is that if a more experienced CEA force is needed, then increasing SRBs is more cost-effective than increasing CSIP. In particular, we find that expanding SRBs yields greater increases in retention than does expanding CSIP for a comparable increase in per capita cost. We also find that to achieve similar increases in retention, expanding CSIP is more expensive than expanding SRBs. The reason is that, unlike SRBs, CSIP does not require a service obligation. Service members can receive CSIP and leave. The service obligation required for receipt of SRBs induces a stronger retention incentive for a given dollar spent than does a policy that increases CSIP.

Our second key conclusion is that the trade-off between increasing SRBs to retain CEAs and increasing accessions to sustain a given CEA force size depends on recruiting and training costs. Available data on recruiting and training costs of CEAs provide estimates of these costs. With the exception of Flight Engineers who are being trained to be part of CV-22 flight crews, we find that it is more cost-effective to increase accessions than to retain CEAs through increases in SRBs. For CV-22 Flight Engineers, our analysis suggests that retaining more experienced personnel using SRBs is more efficient than increasing accessions to sustain a force size when SRB multipliers are less than 2.5, whereas increasing accessions is more efficient if SRB multipliers are above 2.5. Given that estimated recruiting and training costs may be subject to error and that these costs could change in the future, we compute training cost tipping points where once training costs exceed these tipping-point values, it becomes more cost-effective to increase SRBs and have a more-experienced CEA force rather than to increase accessions to maintain force size. These tipping-point calculations do not include the cost of increasing training capacity or the cost of absorbing additional junior personnel into the force. With the exception of Flight Engineers on CV-22 aircraft, estimated recruiting and training costs would have to increase substantially before they exceed these tipping cost values, as show in Table 4.1. For CV-22 Flight Engineers, estimated recruiting and training costs are sufficiently close to the AFSC's estimated tipping point that increasing SRBs and increasing accessions to sustain a given force size cost could be considered approximately the same. This finding suggests that the Air Force could be indifferent between the two options from a cost standpoint.

Table 4.1. Comparison of Recruiting and Training Costs and Tipping Points, by Career Enlisted Aviator Occupation, 2018

Career Enlisted Aviator	Estimated Recruiting and Training Costs	Tipping Points
In-Flight Refueling (1A0)	$289,805	$585,000
Flight Engineers (1A1)	$251,583 (C-130H) to $1,559,003 (CV-22)	$1,485,000
Aircraft Loadmasters (1A2)	$113,692 (C-130J) to $316,301 (C-17)	$580,000
Airborne Mission Systems Operators (1A3)	$47,964	$720,000
Airborne Cryptologists (1A8X1)	$85,812 (Spanish) to $194,024 (Arabic)	$1,015,000
Special Missions Aviation (1A9)	$36,402	$1,500,000

NOTES: Estimated recruiting and training costs come from Table 18-1a and Table 35-1 in AFI 65-503 and are scaled up to 2018 dollars. At training costs above the tipping points, it would be more cost-effective to retain CEAs rather than to increase accessions, assuming that SRB Zone A and B multipliers are within the range listed in Table 3.3. At training costs below the tipping points, it would be more cost-effective to increase accessions rather than retain CEAs, assuming that SRB Zone A and B multipliers are within the listed range.

Appendix A. Background on Career Enlisted Aviator Occupations and Special and Incentive Pays

This appendix draws from Chapter 2 and Appendix A of Tong et al. (2020) to provide background on the CEA occupations, the training and experiences required to become mission ready, and S&I pays relevant to these occupations. Additional information can be found in that document. The information from this appendix and from Tong et al. (2020) assists us with the DRM analysis shown in the main text in several ways. First, understanding the responsibilities of each CEA AFSC and the general requirements to become mission ready allows us to determine whether certain subgroups of CEA AFSCs should be modeled together or separately, based on whether the years of prior experience required before becoming mission ready are similar or different. Second, this information also allows us to ensure that the retention profiles seen in the personnel data make sense. In particular, the retention profiles of career fields that require prior experience should not show attrition out of active duty until after they become mission ready. Third, background information on S&I pays tells us the frequency at which each pay is disbursed (monthly, lump sum, installments, etc.) and assists us with determining whether the S&I pays observed in the administrative data are consistent with how these pays are supposed to be distributed. Finally, the description of S&I pays provide us with the background needed to extend the CEA model discussed in main text.

Descriptions of Career Enlisted Aviators

The ten CEA AFSCs listed in Table 1.1 are described briefly below, drawing from information from the relevant Air Force Career Field Education and Training Plan (CFETP).[15] The five-digit AFSC codes are listed after each career title in Table 1.1. The first three digits and the fifth digit designate the CEA career field. The fourth digit represents the skill level. For instance, an in-flight refueling specialist with an AFSC of 1A031 means that they are at the 3-level, that is, the apprentice level, of their career field. Since the subsequent discussion applies to all skill levels, the fourth digit is designated as "X."

In-Flight Refueling (Boom Operators), 1A0X1

In-flight refueling specialists' primary responsibility is to operate fuel boom controls on tanker aircraft. Aside from operating the boom controls, specialists conduct equipment checks

[15] A CFETP for an AFSC is a career path guide. It identifies education and training requirements and resources to meet those requirements for each stage of a career in that AFSC.

and flight inspections, communicate with the tanker pilot and receiving aircraft during refueling, and complete other aircrew and staff functions (U.S. Air Force, 2016a, p. 9).

Flight Engineer, 1A1X1

Flight engineers conduct visual and flight inspections of aircraft, operate and monitor aircraft panels and indicators, compute and record performance analytics and maintain other aircraft records, and perform other administrative and managerial duties related to flight engineer functions (U.S. Air Force, 2016b, p. 9).

Aircraft Loadmaster, 1A2X1

Aircraft loadmasters supervise cargo load planning and placement, operate aircraft winches, brief and direct passengers, airdrop personnel and cargo, and conduct other tasks related to cargo and passenger operations (U.S. Air Force, 2016c, p. 9).

Airborne Mission Systems Operator, 1A3X1

Airborne mission systems operators are tasked with operating and maintaining electronic systems on aircraft, including communications, sensors, on-board computers, and electronic protection systems (U.S. Air Force, 2016d, p. 9).

Flight Attendant, 1A6X1

Flight attendants are responsible for various cabin duties, including demonstrating safety and emergency procedures, preparing and serving meals and beverages, and assisting with loading and unloading passengers and cargo (U.S. Air Force, 2016e, p. 9).

Airborne Cryptologic Language Analyst, 1A8X1

Airborne cryptologic language analysts operate airborne signals intelligence equipment and translate and analyze audio communications. They also process communications on the ground (U.S. Air Force, 2016h, p. 11).

Airborne Intelligence, Surveillance, and Reconnaissance (ISR) Operator, 1A8X2

Airmen in this career field operate airborne ISR systems on certain Air Force aircraft and on similar ground systems. Their tasks include recording, analyzing, and disseminating ISR information, providing ISR threat warnings, and coordinating with other units (U.S. Air Force, 2012, p. 10).

Special Missions Aviation, 1A9X1

Airmen in the special missions aviation career field are responsible for a diverse set of tasks on special operations aircraft that are similar in nature to those of loadmasters, engineers, and mission systems operators on other aircraft. They perform in-flight inspections, monitor panels and indicators, assist with cargo and passenger loading and airdrop, and provide weapons defense (U.S. Air Force, 2016f, p. 9).

RPA Sensor Operator, 1U0X1

RPA sensor operators monitor aircraft and weapon systems for remotely piloted aircraft (RPA) and control airborne sensors, such as cameras, to track targets and provide battle damage assessment (U.S. Air Force, 2016g, p. 9).

Enlisted RPA Pilot, 1U1XX

The RPA pilot career field is very new, and, as a result, not only do we not have retention data for this group of CEAs but there also is no CFETP for this career field. The Enlisted Pilot Initial Class started training in October 2016, and the first Enlisted Remotely Piloted Aircraft Pilot Selection Board made selections in February 2017 (Bailey, 2017).

Training and Experience Requirements for Mission Ready Status

The requirements to become a CEA are more stringent than the general requirements to enlist in the Air Force, and the specific requirements differ across the CEA fields. For most CEA fields, airmen must have normal color vision and depth perception, Class III medical standards (as defined in AFI 48-123), height between 64 and 77 inches, no fear of flying, U.S. citizenship and eligibility for a Secret clearance, and an eligibility and willingness to deploy worldwide (AFI 11-402, 2020, pp. 38, 43). Exceptions to these general requirements are listed in the career field sections below.

When they enlist, CEAs, like all enlisted personnel, have the option of enlisting for a four- or six-year term of active duty service (AFI 36-2002, 2017, p. 19). All new enlisted personnel must complete 7.5 weeks of Basic Military Training (AFSC 9T0XX) and an additional period of training called airmen's week, which is designed to give them basic life, leadership, and professional skills to help them transition to their technical training for their various AFSCs. After the completion of these 8.5 weeks, or after transferring from another non-CEA career field, CEA trainees must complete a 23-day Aircrew Fundamentals Course with physiological training at Lackland Air Force Base, Texas, which is then followed by an initial skills course for their career. Note that RPA sensor operators do not complete the physiological training portion of the Aircrew Fundamentals Course. Retrainees from other CEA career fields would almost always begin at the initial skills course.

Typically, CEAs will be awarded the apprentice 3-level AFSC that corresponds with their career field after they successfully complete their initial skills course. Before this point, they would have the basic trainee AFSC, 9T000, or the AFSC of the career field from which they cross-trained. The initial skills courses which award the AFSC for each CEA field and all following training are detailed in the individual CEA sections in the Appendix A in Tong et al. (2020).

After initial skills training, CEA take a series of training courses that are specific to each career field (initial qualification training, mission qualification training, and any prerequisites like survival, evasion, resistance, and escape [SERE] or water survival.) After completion of these courses, CEAs are considered mission ready and are awarded the journeyman 5-level AFSC (USAF, 2016d, p. 18).

Flight engineers and flight attendants are different from the other CEA AFSCs in that they generally have had additional previous experience in other career fields, causing them to have different retention profiles compared with other CEAs. In particular, to enter the flight engineer AFSC, a service member must have one of the following qualifications (AFI 11-421, 2018, p. 18):

- prior 5- or 7-level qualifications in the 1A0, 1A2, 1A3, 1A9, 2AX (Avionics Test Station and Components, Avionics Systems, Aerospace Maintenance, Aerospace Propulsion, or Aircraft Metals Technology), 2M0 (Missile Maintenance), 2T3 (Vehicle Maintenance), or 3E0 (Electrical Systems) AFSCs
- a Federal Aviation Administration (FAA) Flight Engineer certificate with jet or turboprop rating
- an FAA airframe and powerplant (A&P) license
- an FAA Aircraft Maintenance Technician (AMT) license.

However, based on the recommended career paths in the CFETP, it seems that nearly all Flight Engineers are retrainees from one of the AFSCs mentioned in the first bullet above (AFI 11-421, 2018, p. 15).

Flight attendants are typically selected from other career fields at the end of their third year of service. The initial skills course for this AFSC is the Basic Flight Attendant (BFA) course. They must then take SERE and Water Survival Training Courses and other courses at their operational unit. They typically complete their initial qualification training (IQT) and mission qualification training (MQT) and become mission ready during the midpoint of their fifth year of service.

Table A.1 outlines the typical YOS when each CEA AFSC has completed their initial skills course, IQT, and MQT and are considered to be mission ready.

Table A.1. Years of Service When Mission Ready, by Career Enlisted Aviator Air Force Specialty Code

CEA AFSC	Year of Service When Mission Ready
1A0X1, In-Flight Refueling	1
1A1X1, Flight Engineer	5–6
1A2X1, Aircraft Loadmaster	1
1A3X1, Airborne Mission Systems Operator	1
1A6X1, Flight Attendant	5–6 prior to 2016, 1.5 years 2016 onward
1A8X1X, Airborne Cryptologic Language Analyst	3
1A8X2, Airborne Intelligence, Surveillance, and Reconnaissance (ISR) Operator	3
1A9X1, Special Missions Aviation	1
1U0X1, RPA Sensor Operator	1
1U1XX, Enlisted RPA Pilot	Unknown

SOURCES: Information provided by Headquarters U.S. Air Force; U.S. Air Force, 2016a, p. 28; U.S. Air Force, 2016c, p. 29; U.S. Air Force, 2016d, p. 29; U.S. Air Force, 2016h. p. 21; U.S. Air Force, 2012b, p. 14; U.S. Air Force, 2016f, p. 32; U.S. Air Force, 2016g, p. 32.

Reassignment to Different Air Force Specialty Codes

After Basic Military Training, enlisted personnel will be assigned their primary AFSC. However, there are some opportunities to change their career field during their enlistment. Understanding the extent to which service members change career fields is important for the modeling of retention profiles because it tells us which career fields require prior experience and the extent to which service members move across career fields. For example, as mentioned above, some career fields, such as Flight Engineers (1A1XX) and Flight Attendants (1A6XX), require prior experience in other AFSCs. However, enlisted personnel may also retrain into other AFSCs that do not require prior experience in another AFSC. The overwhelming majority (over 90 percent) of service members with a CEA AFSC recorded during their military tenure only have one CEA AFSC on their service record, based on our secondary data analysis, suggesting that movement across CEA AFSCs is rare.

Another reason for enlisted members to change their AFSCs is in response to an Air Force need to balance manpower across career fields. Each year, the Air Force Personnel Center advertises AFSCs that have a surplus ("objective-out") or shortage ("objective-in") of airmen (AFI 36-2626, 2015, p. 12). Eligible members who are in objective-out AFSCs may volunteer to retrain into an objective-in AFSC and may be subject to involuntary retraining to meet Air Force needs. Conversely, enlisted personnel in AFSCs on the objective-in list cannot apply for retraining into other career fields (AFI 36-2626, 2015, p. 19).

Note that first-term airmen (FTA)—that is, enlisted personnel on their first term of enlistment who have not yet agreed to reenlist—are typically not subject to involuntary retraining while in an objective-out AFSC (AFI 36-2626, 2015, pp. 12, 18). However, first-term airmen may voluntarily retrain into other AFSCs via the FTA Retraining Program in between their 35th and 43rd months of enlistment for airmen in a standard four-year enlistment (59th through 67th for six-year enlistees), or nine to 15 months prior to their date of estimated return from overseas for airmen stationed outside of the continental United States (AFI 36-2626, 2015, p. 20). First-term airmen in this program are typically retrained into objective-in AFSCs, but a few first-term airmen may train into other AFSCs that are not facing critical shortages (AFI 36-2626, 2015, p. 20).

In addition to the FTA Retraining Program, there are other special programs that allow second-term airmen, career airmen, airmen disqualified from their current career field, and airmen in other special circumstances to apply for retraining into other AFSCs (AFI 36-2626, 2015, pp. 21–22).

Even when airmen do not retrain, there are instances where the Air Force has created new AFSCs or disbanded old ones. In October 2012, all the airmen in the aerial gunner AFSC (1A7XX) were merged with flight engineers (1A1XX) on rotary aircraft and loadmasters (1A2XX) on AC-130s to create the new Special Missions Aviation AFSC (1A9X1) ("New AFSC Merges Certain Gunners, Engineers, Loadmasters," 2012). The 1A7XX AFSC was disbanded. In November 2014, all but 84 airmen from the airborne operations AFSC (1A4X1) were absorbed by airborne mission systems (1A3X1; Hendrix, 2015). The remainder, consisting of operators on AC-130 gunships, were absorbed by 1A9X1.

Career Enlisted Aviator Special and Incentive Pays

The special pays, incentive pays, and bonuses available to men and women in the armed services are outlined in 37 U.S.C. §§ 301–374. Concise descriptions of the basic qualifications for these special pays, incentive pays, and bonuses can be found in Tong et al. (2020). More detailed, lengthy qualifications can be found in DoD's *Financial Management Regulation* (Office of the Under Secretary of Defense [Comptroller], 2018) or in the respective AFIs for the bonus or special pay; however, the vast majority of airmen who meet the basic requirements below for each pay will receive that pay. There are other special pays, incentive pays, and bonuses that may be offered to airmen from time to time (for instance, a bonus to transfer between military services); however, the following sections detail only those bonuses which are currently offered to airmen in the Career Enlisted Aviator AFSCs.

All special pays, incentive pays, and bonuses included in this document are subject to federal income tax (Internal Revenue Service [IRS], 2018, p. 4) but not federal payroll tax (OUSD[C], 2016, pp. 45-3–45-4).[16] However, all of a CEA's military compensation that is earned during a

[16] American workers pay two types of taxes on their wages: payroll tax and income tax. Payroll taxes are paid automatically from every worker's paycheck, and, generally, all workers owe the same percentage of their wages. These taxes are typically used by federal and state governments to fund social insurance programs. Income tax is also withheld from each paycheck, but the percentage of earnings withheld and ultimately paid may vary significantly between employees due to many factors as these function as prepayments of the income tax burden that the individual worker owes on an annual basis. Although some states assess additional payroll taxes, the federal

month in which a service member was in active duty service in a combat zone or qualified hazardous duty area is exempt from federal income tax (IRS, 2018, p. 12). For example, a CEA who accepts a reenlistment bonus during a month in which he spent a day in a combat zone will not pay any income tax on that bonus or any other pay earned during that month. This exclusion has no dollar limit for enlisted members (IRS, 2018, p. 12). Note, however, that military basic pay earned in a CZ is subject to payroll tax (IRS, 2017).

Table A.2 lists the S&I pays offered to CEAs, including indicators for whether these pays were offered in fiscal year 2018, the pay rates, statutory maximums, eligibility criteria, and frequency of payment. Table A.3 documents S&I pay eligibility by CEA AFSC from 1990 to present.

---

payroll taxes are the Federal Insurance Contributions Act (FICA) taxes, which are used to fund Social Security and Medicare. Workers currently pay 6.2 percent of their wages for Social Security and 1.45 percent of their wages for Medicare under FICA, although the Social Security payroll tax is only paid on the first $128,400 of wage earnings (Social Security Administration, 2017).

Table A.2. Summary of Special and Incentive Pays Available to Career Enlisted Aviators, Fiscal Year 2018

Name	Offered in FY 2018	Rate	Statutory Maximum	Eligibility	Payment
Critical Skills Incentive Pay (formerly Career Enlisted Flyer Incentive Pay)	Yes	\$225–\$600/month	\$1,000/month	Based on AFSC (1AXXX and 1UXXX), frequency of aviation service, and YAS.	Continuous monthly pay may become conditional (eligibility determined each month) at year 10
Remotely Piloted Aircraft Enlisted Aviation Incentive Pay	No	\$150–\$400/month (may not exceed \$1,500/month in combination with other aviation incentive pay)	\$3,000/month (all AIP)	Based on AFSC (1U0X1), frequency of aviation service, and YAS.	Continuous monthly pay may become conditional (eligibility determined each month) at year 10
Hazardous Duty Incentive Pay (crew member)	Yes	\$150–\$240/month	\$150–\$240/month	Rate based on rank, pay requires "regular and frequent" flying duty as crew member. May not be received with CSIP (formerly CEFIP).	Conditional (eligibility determined each month)
Foreign Language Proficiency Pay	Yes	\$125–\$1,000/month	\$1000/month	Based on language and skill level. Eligibility is redetermined through language testing every two years.	Continuous monthly pay
Special Duty Assignment Pay	Yes	\$150–\$375/month	\$600/month	May be based on AFSC, aircraft, unit, qualification, or time in place.	Continuous monthly pay
Selective Reenlistment Bonus	Yes	monthly basic pay × multiplier × years reenlisting (multipliers range from 2–6, minimum commitment is 3 years)	\$90,000 total	Offered to certain career fields with high training costs or low retention rates.	Minimum of 50% of total paid at reenlistment signing, with remainder paid in equal annual installations
Hostile Fire Pay/ Imminent Danger Pay (IDP)	Yes	\$225/month	\$225/month	Flat rate paid if assigned to IDP designated area or exposed to hostile fire.	Conditional (must meet eligibility each month)
Hardship Duty Pay—Location	Yes	\$50–\$150/month	\$1,500/month	Based on assignment location.	Continuous monthly pay
Assignment Incentive Pay (AIP)	Yes	\$300–\$900/month	\$3,000/month (all AIP)	May be based on location, time in place, and nature of assignment (voluntary/involuntary).	Continuous monthly pay
Enlistment Bonus	Yes	\$6,000 total	\$40,000 total	May be offered to career fields with critical shortages. Currently offered only to 1A8X1 for 6-year contracts.	Typically paid in lump sum at completion of tech school

SOURCES: **CSIP**—AFI 11-401, 2018, pp. 1, 35, 37, 76; OUSD(C), 2018, pp. 22–25; **HDIP**—AFI 11-421, 2018, p. 87; AFI 11-401, 2018, pp. 34, 76; DoD, Office of the Under Secretary of Defense for Personnel and Readiness (OUSD[P&R]), 2011, p. 268; DoD, Military Compensation Policy, "Hazardous Duty Incentive Pay (HDIP)," webpage, undated-b; **RPA CEAVIP**—OUSD(C), 2016, pp. 22–28; 37 U.S.C. § 307(a); AFI 11-421, 2018, p. 2; **FLPP**—AFI 36-4002, 2015b, pp. 10–13; Office of the Under Secretary of Defense for Personnel and Readiness (OUSD[P&R]), 2011, pp. 555–557; **SDAP**—DoD, Military Compensation Policy, undated-e; Headquarters U.S. Air Force, phone communication, June 1, 2018; OUSD(P&R), 2011, p. 539; **SRB**—AFI 36-2606, 2017, pp. 45–49; OUSD(P&R), 2011, pp. 509–511. **HFP/IDP**—OUSD(P&R), 2011, pp. 235–237; "Hostile Fire/Imminent Danger Pay" in OUSD(C), 2018; **HDP**—DoD, Military Compensation Policy, undated-e; OUSD(P&R), 2011, pp. 548–549; **AIP**—OUSD(P&R), 2011, pp. 543–549; AFI 36-2110, 2018, p. 331; DoD, Military Compensation Policy, undated-a; **EB**—OUSD(P&R), 2011, pp. 496–499; Headquarters U.S. Air Force, phone communication, June 1, 2018.

Table A.3. Special and Incentive Pay Eligibility Among Career Enlisted Aviators, 1990 to Present

CEA AFSC Code	Description	Critical Skills Incentive Pay (CSIP)	Hazardous Duty Incentive Pay (HDIP)	RPF Career Enlisted Aviation Incentive Pay (RPA CEAVIP)	Foreign Language Proficiency Bonus (FLPB)	Special Duty Assignment Pay (SDAP)	Selective Reenlistment Bonus	Hostile Fire/ Imminent Danger Pay (HFP/IDP)	Hardship Duty Pay (HDP)	Assignment Incentive Pay (AIP)	Enlistment Bonus (EB)
1A0X1	In-Flight Refueling (boom operators)	CSIP replaced Career Enlisted Flyer Incentive Pay (CEFIP) on Oct. 1, 2017. CEFIP was created in 1999. 1AXXX AFSCs were eligible for CEFIP beginning in 1999 and are currently eligible for CSIP; Service members receive the greater of CSIP and Hazardous Duty Pay	Eligible if not receiving CSIP and if CEA has completed at least 4 hours of qualifying flight time in that month.	Not eligible	Eligible	Not eligible	Eligibility varies by year, AFSC, and sometimes subgroups within AFSC.	Eligible if assigned to an IDP area or on-board an aircraft near hostile fire at any point during a month	Location-based pay to compensate for experiencing a quality of life significantly below that of the U.S.	Location-based pay established in 2002 to compensate airmen for serving in undesirable locations (e.g., Iraq, Korea, Kuwait, Turkey)	Eligibility varies by year and AFSC. Offered to career fields with critical shortages.
1A1X1	Flight Engineers			Not eligible		Eligible if on: (1) MC-130H or AC-130U/J/W after IQT or after obtaining instructor qualification (2) any aircraft at certain units (designated by Personnel Accounting Symbol codes)					
1A2X1	Aircraft Loadmaster			Not eligible		Eligible if on: (1) HC-130J, MC-130J, or MC-130H after IQT or after obtaining instructor qualification (2) any aircraft at certain units (designated by Personnel Accounting Symbol codes)					
1A3X1	Airborne Mission Systems Operator			Not eligible		Eligible if on: (1) any aircraft at certain units (designated by Personnel Accounting Symbol codes)					
1A6X1	Flight Attendant			Not eligible		Not eligible					
1A8X1	Airborne Cryptologist			Not eligible		Not eligible					
1A8X2	Airborne ISR Operator			Not eligible		Not eligible					
1A9X1	Special Mission Aviation			Not eligible		Eligible if on: (1) AC-130U/J/W, CV-22, MI-17, T/UH-1D/F/N, or HH-60 aircraft after IQT or after obtaining instructor qualification (2) CV-22 after obtaining lead flight engineer certification or after obtaining instructor qualification (3) any aircraft at certain units (designated by Personnel Accounting Symbol codes)					
1U0X1	RPA Sensor Operator			Eligible since Dec. 22, 2014; Replaced by CSIP Oct. 1, 2018		Eligible if on: (1) MQ-1 or MQ-9 after IQT or after obtaining instructor qualification					
1U1XX	Enlisted RPA Pilot	Eligible for CSIP beginning Oct. 1, 2017; Receive the greater of CSIP and Hazardous Duty Pay		Not eligible		Not eligible					

SOURCES: **CSIP**—OUSD(C), 2018, pp. 1, 16–26; AFI 11-421, 2018, p. 87; 37 U.S.C. § 320; **RPA CEAVIP**—OUSD(C), 2016, pp. 27–28; OUSD(C), 2018, p. 1; **FLPB**—AFI 36-4002, 2015b, pp. 4–13; **SDAP**—information provided by Headquarters U.S. Air Force, 2018; **SRB**—AFI 36-2606, 2017, pp. 42–53; **HFP/IDP**—DoD, Military Compensation Policy, undated-d; **HDP**—DoD, Military Compensation Policy, undated-c; **AIP**—DoD, Military Compensation Policy, undated-a; OUSD(P&R), 2011, p. 543; **EB**—OUSD(P&R), 2011, p. 498; **HDIP**—AFI 11-401, 2018, pp. 34, 76.

Appendix B. Retention Profiles of Career Enlisted Aviators

This appendix shows the retention profiles of each CEA AFSC modeled in this report. The switching costs included in each model is based on these retention profiles.

Figure B.1. In-Flight Refueling (1A0) Observed Active and Reserve Component Retention

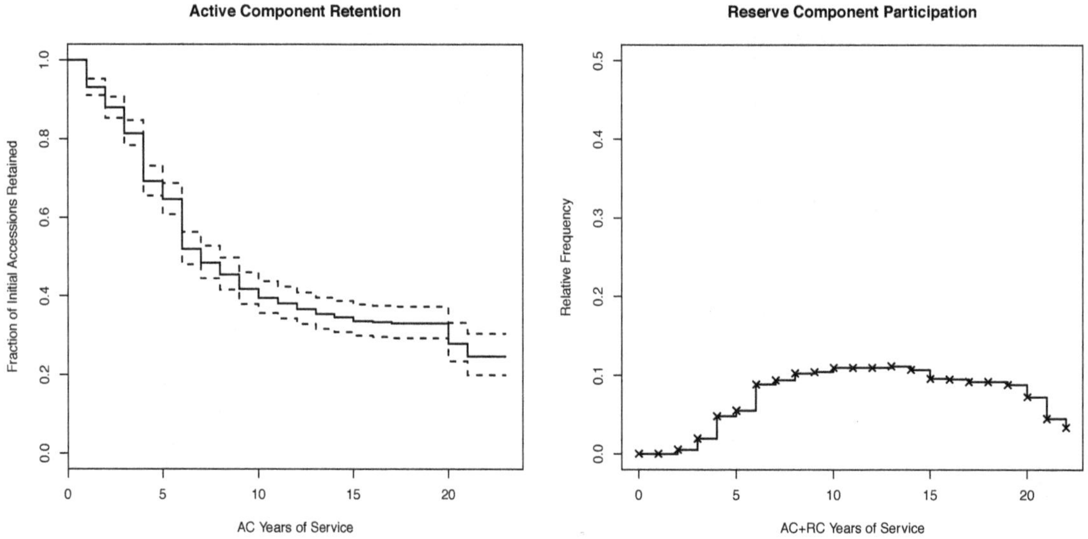

SOURCE: Authors' computations.

Figure B.2. Flight Engineers (1A1) Observed Active and Reserve Component Retention

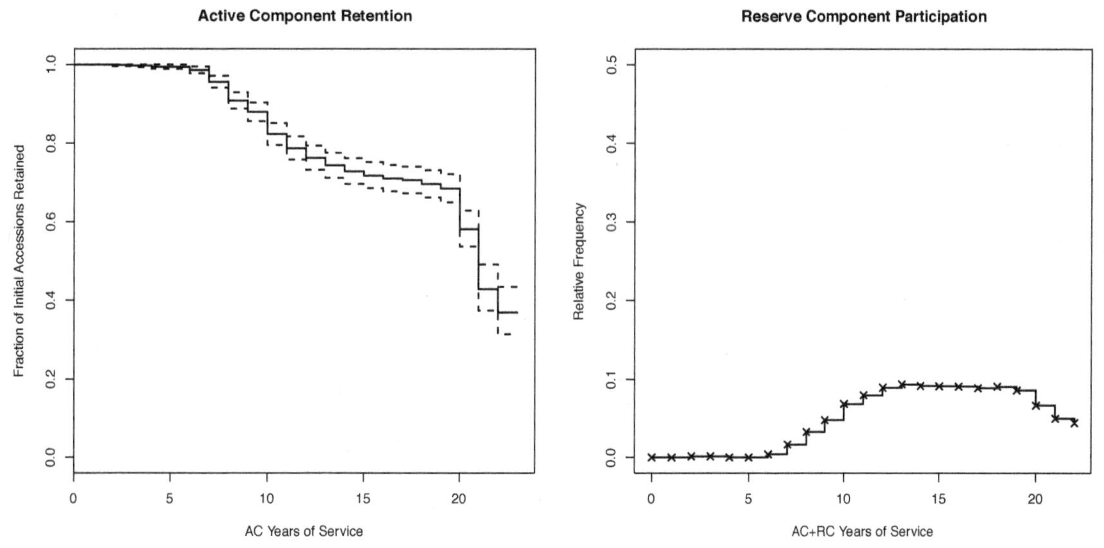

SOURCE: Authors' computations.

Figure B.3. Aircraft Loadmasters (1A2) Observed Active and Reserve Component Retention

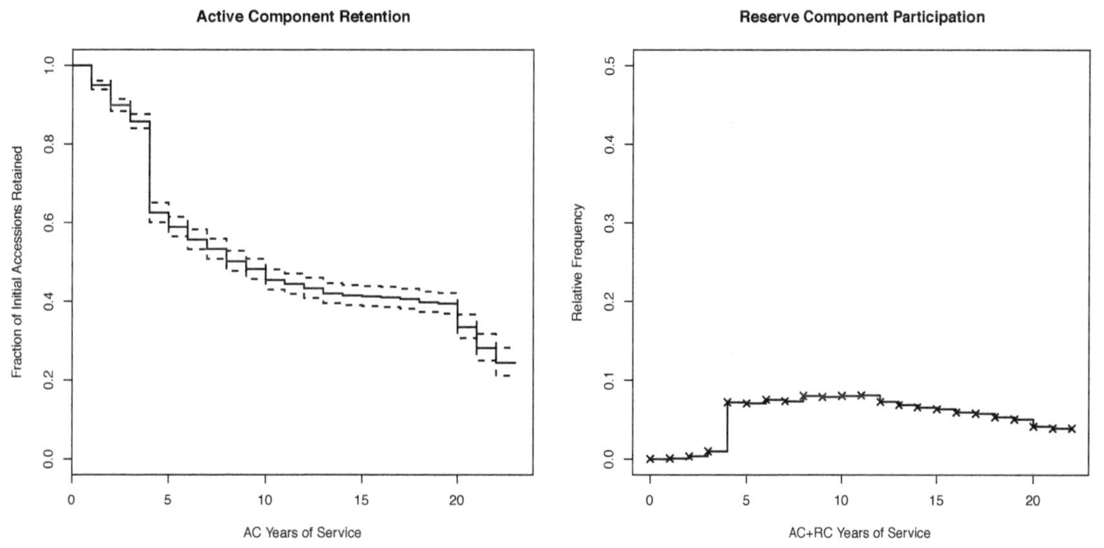

SOURCE: Authors' computations.

Figure B.4. Airborne Mission Systems Operators (1A3) Observed Active and Reserve Component Retention

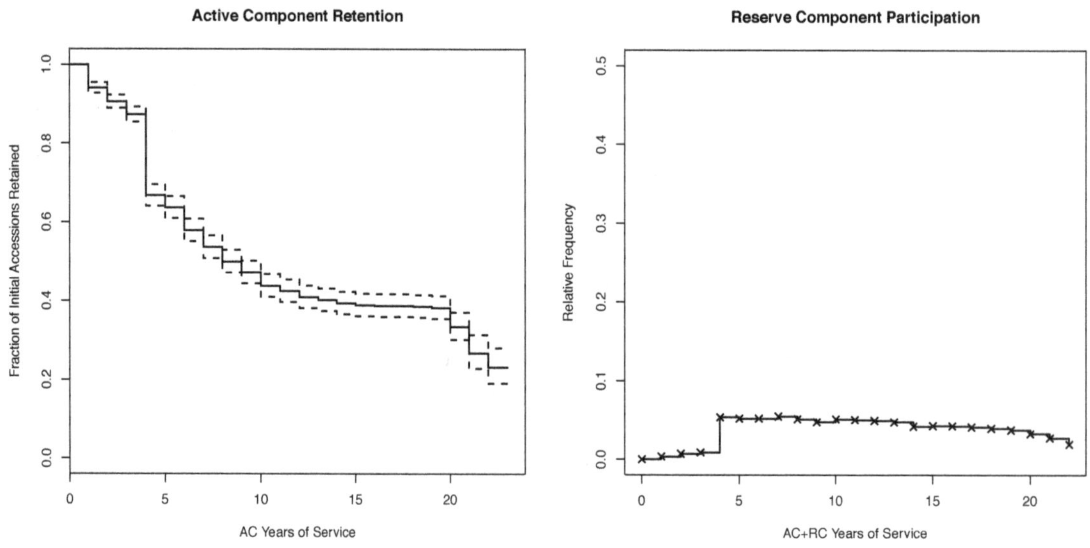

SOURCE: Authors' computations.

Figure B.5. Airborne Cryptologists (1A8X1) Observed Active and Reserve Component Retention

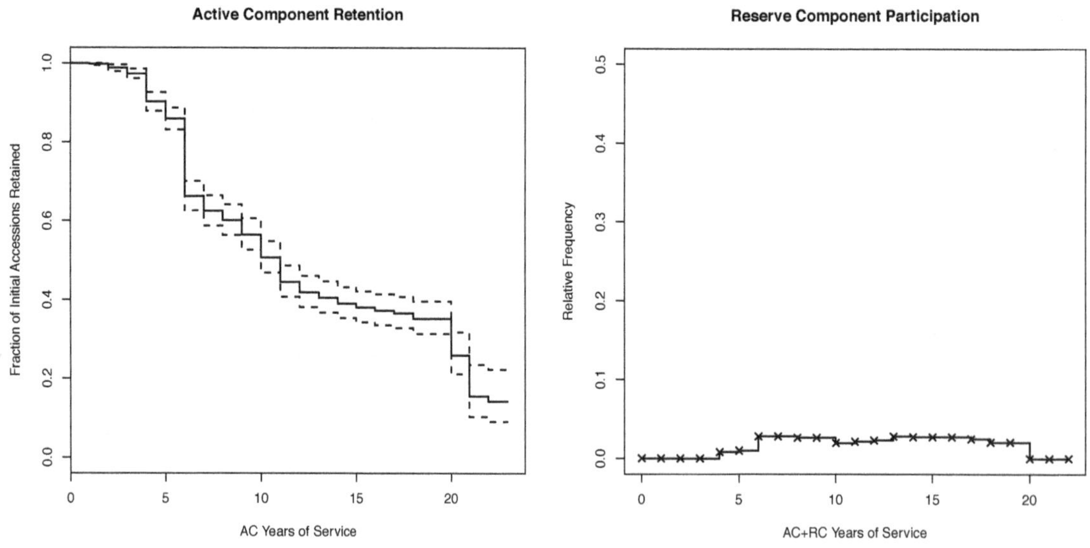

SOURCE: Authors' computations.

Figure B.6. Special Missions Aviation (1A9) Observed Active and Reserve Component Retention

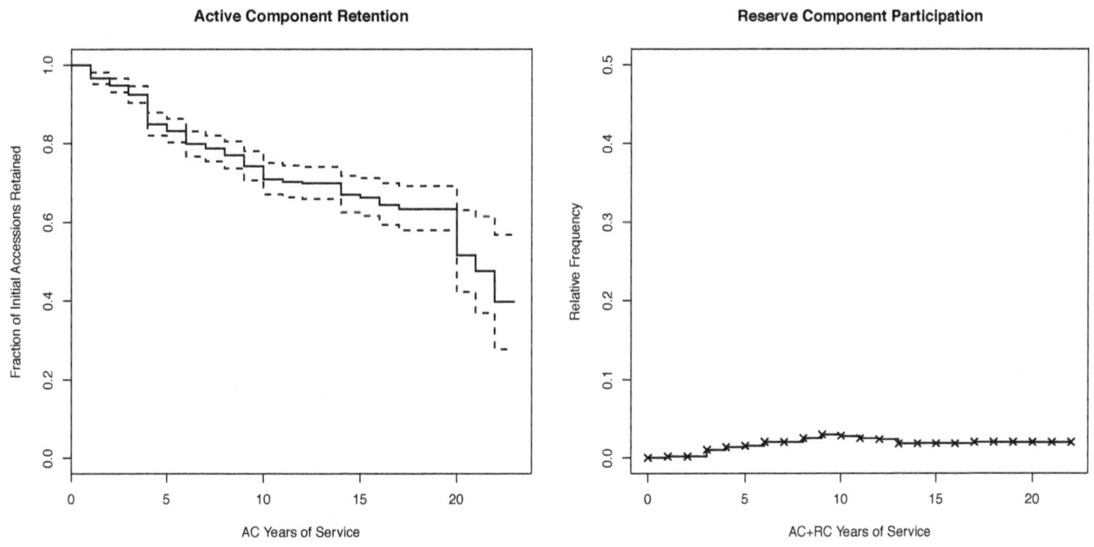

SOURCE: Authors' computations.

Figure B.7. RPA Sensor Operators (1U0) Observed Active and Reserve Component Retention

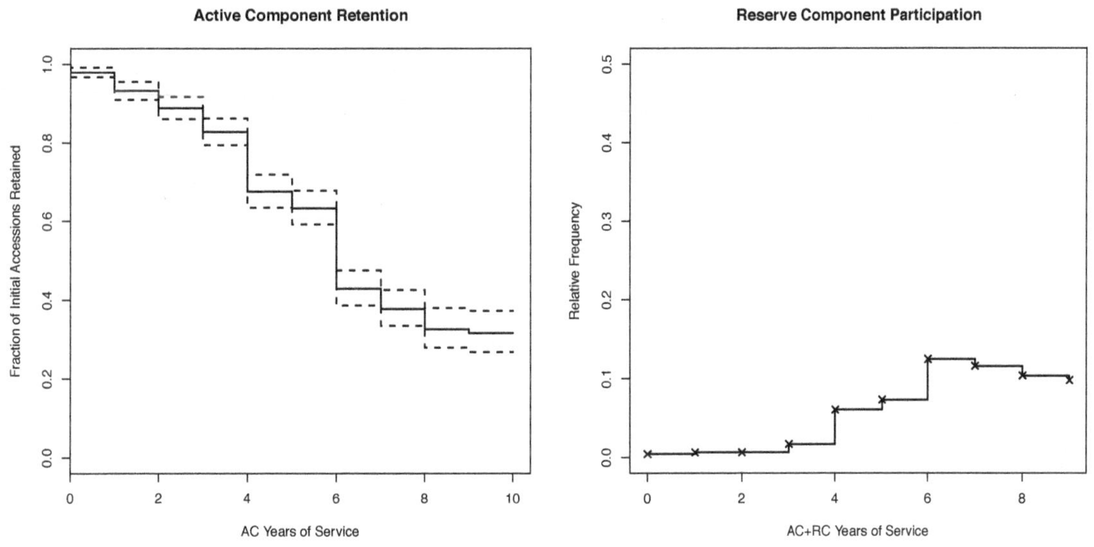

SOURCE: Authors' computations.

Appendix C. Simulations of the Retention and Cost Effects of Alternative Special and Incentive Pay Policies

This appendix shows the simulated effects of different S&I policy on retention and per capita costs.

Table C.1. Simulations with Different Special and Incentive Pays, Flight Engineers (1A1)

	% Increase in Retention	% Increase in Retention, Less Than 10 YOS	% Increase in Per Capita Cost
$1000 CSIP at < 10 YOS	2.3	0.7	4.5
Replace CSIP with AvIP	13.7	1.6	7.7
$1000 CSIP at all YOS	18.9	1.8	13.5
SRB Zone A & B Multipliers = 6	10.3	1.9	5.7
SRB Zone A & B Multipliers = 7	11.2	2.1	6.7
SRB Zone A & B Multipliers = 8	11.9	2.2	7.6

SOURCE: Authors' computations.
NOTES: Percentage changes are relative to a baseline with CSIP rates as of October 1, 2017, and SRB multipliers as of July 31, 2019.

Table C.2. Simulations with Different Special and Incentive Pays, Aircraft Loadmasters (1A2)

	% Increase in Retention	% Increase in Retention, Less Than 10 YOS	% Increase in Per Capita Cost
$1000 CSIP at < 10 YOS	11.4	10.4	4.6
Replace CSIP with AvIP	18.3	7.4	7.0
$1000 CSIP at all YOS	30.9	14.0	12.8
SRB Zone A & B Multipliers = 6	13.5	9.0	3.5
SRB Zone A & B Multipliers = 7	17.2	11.7	4.5
SRB Zone A & B Multipliers = 8	20.1	14.0	5.5

SOURCE: Authors' computations.
NOTES: Percentage changes are relative to a baseline with CSIP rates as of October 1, 2017, and SRB multipliers as of July 31, 2019.

Table C.3. Simulations with Different Special and Incentive Pays, Airborne Mission Systems Operators (1A3)

	% Increase in Retention	% Increase in Retention, Less Than 10 YOS	% Increase in Per Capita Cost
$1000 CSIP at < 10 YOS	12.8	10.7	5.9
Replace CSIP with AvIP	19.5	7.4	7.7
$1000 CSIP at all YOS	32.6	14.8	14.3
SRB Zone A & B Multipliers = 6	30.9	17.6	8.6
SRB Zone A & B Multipliers = 7	34.6	19.9	9.8
SRB Zone A & B Multipliers = 8	37.9	22.1	10.9

SOURCE: Authors' computations.
NOTES: Percentage changes are relative to a baseline with CSIP rates as of October 1, 2017, and SRB multipliers as of July 31, 2019.

Table C.4. Simulations with Different Special and Incentive Pays, Airborne Cryptologists (1A8X1)

	% Increase in Retention	% Increase in Retention, Less Than 10 YOS	% Increase in Per Capita Cost
$1000 CSIP at < 10 YOS	6.7	3.8	6.1
Replace CSIP with AvIP	11.8	3.3	6.8
$1000 CSIP at all YOS	17.2	5.4	12.4
SRB Zone A & B Multipliers = 6	3.0	1.0	1.0
SRB Zone A & B Multipliers = 7	5.5	2.2	2.5
SRB Zone A & B Multipliers = 8	7.8	3.3	3.8

SOURCE: Authors' computations.
NOTES: Percentage changes are relative to a baseline with CSIP rates as of October 1, 2017, and SRB multipliers as of July 31, 2019.

Table C.5. Simulations with Different Special and Incentive Pays, Special Missions Aviation (1A9)

	% Increase in Retention	% Increase in Retention, Less Than 10 YOS	% Increase in Per Capita Cost
$1000 CSIP at < 10 YOS	2.3	1.7	3.4
Replace CSIP with AVIP	4.4	1.4	5.4
$1000 CSIP at all YOS	7.8	2.2	10.1
SRB Zone A & B Multipliers = 6	2.5	1.6	2.5
SRB Zone A & B Multipliers = 7	3.0	1.8	3.2
SRB Zone A & B Multipliers = 8	3.4	2.1	4.0

SOURCE: Authors' computations.
NOTES: Percentage changes are relative to a baseline with CSIP rates as of October 1, 2017, and SRB multipliers as of July 31, 2019.

References

AFI—*See* Air Force Instruction.

Air Force Instruction 11-401, *Aviation Management*, Washington, D.C.: Department of the Air Force, February 14, 2018.

Air Force Instruction 11-402, *Aviation and Parachutist Service*, Washington, D.C.: Department of the Air Force, February 12, 2020.

Air Force Instruction 11-421, *Aviation Resource Management*, Washington, D.C.: Department of the Air Force, February 14, 2018.

Air Force Instruction 36-2002, *Enlisted Accessions*, Washington, D.C.: Department of the Air Force, 2017.

Air Force Instruction 36-2110, *Assignments*, Washington, D.C.: Department of the Air Force, October 5, 2018

Air Force Instruction 36-2606, *Reenlistment and Extension of Enlistment in the United States Air Force*, Washington, D.C.: Department of the Air Force, July 27, 2017.

Air Force Instruction 36-2626, *Airman Retraining Program*, Washington, D.C.: Department of the Air Force, June 3, 2015.

Air Force Instruction 36-4002, *Air Force Foreign Language Proficiency Bonus Program*, Washington, D.C.: Department of the Air Force, June 16, 2015.

Air Force Instruction 48-123, *Medical Examinations and Standards*, Washington, D.C.: Department of the Air Force, November 5, 2013.

Air Force Instruction 65-503, *U.S. Air Force Cost and Planning Factors*, Washington, D.C.: Department of the Air Force, July 13, 2018.

Air Force Personnel Center, "Regular Air Force Selective Retention Bonus Listing," effective July 31, 2019.

Asch, Beth J., James Hosek, Michael G. Mattock, and Christina Panis, *Assessing Compensation Reform: Research in Support of the 10th Quadrennial Review of Military Compensation*, Santa Monica, Calif.: RAND Corporation, MG-764-OSD, 2008. As of December 1, 2019: http://www.rand.org/pubs/monographs/MG764.html

Asch, Beth J., James Hosek, and Michael G. Mattock, *A Policy Analysis of Reserve Retirement Reform*, Santa Monica, Calif.: RAND Corporation, MG-378-OSD, 2013. As of December 1,

2019:
https://www.rand.org/pubs/monographs/MG378.html

Bailey, Kat, "Enlisted RPA Pilot Board Selects 30 Airmen for Pilot Training," Air Force News Service, March 8, 2017. As of February 18, 2018:
http://www.557weatherwing.af.mil/DesktopModules/ArticleCS/Print.aspx?PortalId=62&ModuleId=11614&Article=1106708

DoD—*See* U.S. Department of Defense.

Hendrix, Torri, "AFSC Merger Ensures Airborne Situational Awareness," U.S. Air Force, June 30, 2015. As of October 6, 2020:
https://www.af.mil/News/Article-Display/Article/602454/afsc-merger-ensures-airborne-situational-awareness/

Hosek, James, Shanthi Nataraj, Michael G. Mattock, and Beth J. Asch, *The Role of Special and Incentive Pays in Retaining Military Mental Health Care Providers*, Santa Monica, Calif.: RAND Corporation, RR-1425-OSD, 2017. As of December 1, 2019:
https://www.rand.org/pubs/research_reports/RR1425.html

Internal Revenue Service, "Tax Exclusion for Combat Service," IRS.gov, August 12, 2017. As of February 23, 2018:
https://www.irs.gov/individuals/military/tax-exclusion-for-combat-service

———, *Publication 3: Armed Forces' Tax Guide*, Washington, D.C.: U.S. Department of the Treasury, Cat. No. 46072M, February 20, 2018. As of February 23, 2018:
https://www.irs.gov/pub/irs-pdf/p3.pdf

IRS—*See* Internal Revenue Service.

Kaplan, E. L., and Paul Meier, "Nonparametric Estimation from Incomplete Observations," *Journal of the American Statistical Association*, Vol. 53, No. 282, 1958, pp. 457–481.

Mattock, Michael G., James Hosek, Beth J. Asch, and Rita Karam, *Retaining U.S. Air Force Pilots When the Civilian Demand for Pilots Is Growing*, Santa Monica, Calif.: RAND Corporation, RR-1455-AF, 2016. As of December 1, 2019:
https://www.rand.org/pubs/research_reports/RR1455.html

Mattock, Michael G., Beth J. Asch, James Hosek, and Michael Boito, *The Relative Cost-Effectiveness of Retaining Versus Accessing Air Force Pilots*, Santa Monica, Calif.: RAND Corporation, RR-2415-AF, 2019. As of December 1, 2019:
https://www.rand.org/pubs/research_reports/RR2415.html

McFadden, Daniel, "Quantitative Methods for Analyzing Travel Behaviour of Individuals: Some Recent Developments," Cowles Foundation Discussion Papers 474, Cowles Foundation for Research in Economics, Yale University, 1977.

"New AFSC Merges Certain Gunners, Engineers, Loadmasters," Air Force News Service, August 6, 2012. As of February 18, 2018: http://www.af.mil/News/Article-Display/Article/110683/new-afsc-merges-certain-gunners-engineers-loadmasters/

Office of the Under Secretary of Defense for Personnel and Readiness, *Military Compensation Background Papers: Compensation Elements and Related Manpower Cost Items, Their Purposes and Legislative Backgrounds*, 7th ed., Washington, D.C., November 2011.

Office of the Under Secretary of Defense for Personnel and Readiness, Directorate of Compensation, *Selected Military Compensation Tables*, 1980–2018.

Office of the Under Secretary of Defense (Comptroller), DoD 7000.14-R, *Department of Defense Financial Management Regulation*, Volume 7A, *Military Pay Policy, Active Duty and Reserve Pay*, Washington, D.C., November 2016. As of December 11, 2019: https://comptroller.defense.gov/FMR.aspx

———, DoD 7000.14-R, *Department of Defense Financial Management Regulation*, Volume 7A, *Military Pay Policy, Active Duty and Reserve Pay*, Washington, D.C., February 2018. As of December 11, 2019: https://comptroller.defense.gov/FMR.aspx

OUSD(C)—*See* Office of the Under Secretary of Defense (Comptroller).

OUSD(P&R)—*See* Office of the Under Secretary of Defense for Personnel and Readiness.

Social Security Administration, "OASDI and SSI Program Rates & Limits, 2018," in *Research, Statistics, & Policy Analysis*, Washington, D.C., November 2017.

Tong, Patricia K., Michael G. Mattock, Beth J. Asch, James Hosek, and Felix Knutson, *Modeling Career Enlisted Aviator Retention in the U.S. Air Force*, Santa Monica, Calif.: RAND Corporation, RR-3134-AF, 2020. As of August 20, 2020: https://www.rand.org/pubs/research_reports/RR3134.html

U.S. Air Force, *Career Field Education and Training Plan 1A8X2X: Airborne Intelligence, Surveillance, and Reconnaissance (ISR) Operator Specialty*, Washington, D.C.: Department of the Air Force, November 1, 2012.

———, *Career Field Education and Training Plan 1A0X1: In-Flight Refueling*, Washington, D.C.: Department of the Air Force, January 19, 2016a.

———, *Career Field Education and Training Plan 1A1X1: Flight Engineer*, Washington, D.C.: Department of the Air Force, January 19, 2016b.

———, *Career Field Education and Training Plan 1A2X1: Aircraft Loadmaster*, Washington, D.C.: Department of the Air Force, January 19, 2016c.

———, *Career Field Education and Training Plan 1A3X1: Airborne Mission Systems Operator*, Washington, D.C.: Department of the Air Force, January 19, 2016d.

———, *Career Field Education and Training Plan 1A6X1: Flight Attendant*, Washington, D.C.: Department of the Air Force, January 19, 2016e.

———, *Career Field Education and Training Plan 1A9X1: Special Missions Aviation*, January 19, 2016f.

———, *Career Field Education and Training Plan 1U0X1: Remotely Piloted Aircraft Sensor Operator (RPA SO)*, Washington, D.C.: Department of the Air Force, January 19, 2016g.

———, *Career Field Education and Training Plan 1A8X1X: Airborne Cryptologic Language Analyst*, Washington, D.C.: Department of the Air Force, March 1, 2016h.

U.S. Code, Title 37: Pay and Allowances of the Uniformed Services; Chapter 5: Special and Incentive Pays; Subchapter I: Existing Special Pay, Incentive Pay, and Bonus Authorities; Section 307: Special Pay: Special Duty Assignment Pay for Enlisted Members. As of July 8, 2019:
https://www.law.cornell.edu/uscode/text/37/307

U.S. Department of Defense, Military Compensation Policy, "Assignment Incentive Pay (AIP)," webpage, undated-a. As of January 25, 2018:
http://militarypay.defense.gov/Pay/Special-and-Incentive-Pays/AIP/

———, "Hazardous Duty Incentive Pay (HDIP)," webpage, undated-b. As of January 25, 2018:
http://militarypay.defense.gov/Pay/Special-and-Incentive-Pays/HDIP/

———, "Hardship Duty Pay (HDP)," webpage, undated-c. As of September 13, 2018:
https://militarypay.defense.gov/Pay/Special-and-Incentive-Pays/HDP/

———, "Hostile Fire/Imminent Danger Pay (HFP/IDP)," webpage, undated-d. As of January 25, 2018:
http://militarypay.defense.gov/Pay/Special-and-Incentive-Pays/HFP_IDP/

———, "Special and Incentive Pay Index," webpage, undated-e. As of January 25, 2018:
http://militarypay.defense.gov/Pay/Special-and-Incentive-Pays/Index/

U.S. Department of Defense, Office of the Actuary, *Valuation of the Military Retirement System, as of September 30, 2017*, April 2019. As of February 19, 2020:
https://media.defense.gov/2019/Apr/26/2002122105/-1/-1/0/MRF%20VALRPT%202017%20[APRIL%202019]%20FINAL.PDF

CPSIA information can be obtained
at www.ICGtesting.com
Printed in the USA
LVHW012003200221
679507LV00009B/799